SOCRATIC STUDIES

SOCRATIC STUDIES

GREGORY VLASTOS

*Formerly Emeritus Professor of Philosophy at Princeton University
and at the University of California at Berkeley*

EDITED BY
MYLES BURNYEAT

*Laurence Professor of Ancient Philosophy in the
University of Cambridge*

CAMBRIDGE
UNIVERSITY PRESS

Published by the Press Syndicate of the University of Cambridge
The Pitt Building, Trumpington Street, Cambridge CB2 1RP
40 West 20th Street, New York, NY 10011-4211 USA
10 Stamford Road, Oakleigh, Melbourne 3166, Australia

© Cambridge University Press 1994

First published 1994
Reprinted 1995

Printed in Great Britain by Athenæum Press Ltd, Gateshead, Tyne & Wear

A catalogue record for this book is available from the British Library

Library of Congress cataloguing in publication data

Vlastos, Gregory.
Socratic studies / Gregory Vlastos; edited by Myles Burnyeat.
p.   cm.
Includes bibliographical references and indexes.
Contents: The Socratic elenchus – Socrates' disavowal of
knowledge – Is the Socratic fallacy Socratic? – The historical
Socrates and Athenian democracy – The Protagoras and the Laches –
Epilogue: Socrates and Vietnam.
ISBN 0 521 44213 3 (hardback) – ISBN 0 521 44735 6 (paperback)
1. Socrates.   I. Burnyeat, Myles.   II. Title.
B317.V57 1994
183'.2–dc20   92-47419   CIP

ISBN 0 521 44213 3 hardback
ISBN 0 521 44735 6 paperback

AO

CONTENTS

EDITOR'S PREFACE

Socratic Studies is the companion volume to Gregory Vlastos' *Socrates: Ironist and Moral Philosopher* (1991). It contains, as promised in the Introduction (pp. 18–19) to that work, revised versions of three previously published essays on Socrates plus some new material. Sadly, not as much new material as he had planned to write.

Chapter 1 derives from "The Socratic Elenchus," *Oxford Studies in Ancient Philosophy* 1 (1983), 27–58. It is the most extensively revised, with some substantial changes and numerous smaller ones. The changes are GV's response to comments and criticisms made in the lively discussion that followed the original publication. The 1983 volume of *Oxford Studies* already contained (at pp. 71–4) GV's "Afterthoughts on the Socratic elenchus," which are here revised, expanded and made consistent with Chapter 1 under the heading "Postscript to 'The Socratic elenchus.'"

In the course of entering corrections and improvements from various dates (the last being 30 January 1991) I have occasionally had to make a decision on whether an omission or change was deliberate or simply a slip in the typing up; I am confident that no point of substance is affected. In the Appendix to Chapter 1 GV started to expand his account of the *Euthydemus*, but only two inconclusive paragraphs were written; these have been omitted. Throughout the book I have checked references and corrected mistakes of citation.

Chapter 2 derives from "Socrates' Disavowal of Knowledge," *Philosophical Quarterly* 35 (1985), 1–31. The major change is the removal of pp. 23–6 on the "Socratic Fallacy," which was superseded by the material that appears here as Chapter 3.

Chapter 3 derives from "Is the 'Socratic Fallacy' Socratic?," *Ancient Philosophy* 10 (1990), 1–16, with minor changes and some additional notes.

Chapter 4 derives from "The Historical Socrates and Athenian Democracy," *Political Theory* 11 (1983), 495–515. Apart from a few corrections, the only change is on the first page: a recasting of the first of the two theses GV will argue for.

Chapter 5 on the *Protagoras* and the *Laches* is entirely new and caused some editorial problems. Readers should be warned that it is not a completely finished piece of work.

(i) In section II(A) GV altered the numbered steps in his analysis of the Terminal Argument in the *Laches* without adjusting the numbers used to refer to them in the subsequent text. I have attempted to straighten things out, in consultation with Alan Code, Terence Irwin, Richard Kraut, David Sedley, and an older draft of the chapter. The result is to some extent conjectural, but I believe that it is faithful to GV's thought.

(ii) It is not made as clear as it might be that, in addition to his main line of argument for dating the *Laches* later than the *Protagoras*, GV is simultaneously, and characteristically, engaged in a dialectical critique of his own earlier self. In the Appendix, "The argument in *La.* 197Eff.," to Chapter 10 of *Platonic Studies*, he urged that the Terminal Argument in the *Laches* is meant to strike the reader as invalid: this allows the Platonic Socrates to hold on to *both* Premise (1), "Courage is knowledge of fearful and confidence-sustaining things," *and* Premise (2), "Courage is a part of virtue." A few years later, in the older draft I have already mentioned, he accepted that the argument is meant to be valid (cf. also *Platonic Studies*, 2nd edn., starred note at pp. 443–5) and resurrected for it his celebrated description of the Third Man Argument in Plato's *Parmenides*: "a record of honest perplexity." The perplexity was about how to adjust Premise (1) to make it compatible with Premise (2), which GV always defended as good Socratic belief. In the new version printed here (dated 18 November 1990) that perplexity is replaced by an answer.

GV planned to round off *Socratic Studies* with a sixth chapter on the *Lysis*. But the work he did for this is not substantial enough to print. The Epilogue "Socrates and Vietnam" which stands here in its place was not part of GV's own conception of the book. But it matches so well the Epilogue "Felix Socrates" in *Socrates: Ironist and Moral Philosopher* that it seemed right to include it.

MFB

ABBREVIATIONS

Ap.	*Apology*
Ch.	*Charmides*
Cr.	*Crito*
Eu.	*Euthyphro*
Eud.	*Euthydemus*
G.	*Gorgias*
HMa.	*Hippias Major*
HMi.	*Hippias Minor*
La.	*Laches*
Lg.	*Laws*
Ly.	*Lysis*
M.	*Meno*
Phd.	*Phaedo*
Pr.	*Protagoras*
R.	*Republic*
Smp.	*Symposium*
Sph.	*Sophist*
Tht.	*Theaetetus*
Ti.	*Timaeus*

PS   G. Vlastos, *Platonic Studies* (2nd edn., Princeton 1981)

Socrates   G. Vlastos, *Socrates: Ironist and Moral Philosopher* (Cambridge and Ithaca 1991)

I

THE SOCRATIC ELENCHUS:
METHOD IS ALL[1]

I

In Plato's earlier dialogues[2] – in all of them except the *Euthydemus*,
Hippias Major, Lysis, Menexenus – Socrates' inquiries display a pattern
of investigation whose rationale he does not investigate. They are
constrained by rules he does not undertake to justify. In marked
contrast to "Socrates" speaking for Plato in the middle dialogues,
who refers repeatedly to the "method" (μέθοδος) he follows (either
in general[3] or for the special purpose of some particular investigation[4]), the "Socrates" who speaks for Socrates in the earlier dialogues never uses this word[5] and never discusses his method of investigation. He never troubles to say why his way of searching is the
way to discover truth or even what this way of searching is. He has

---

[1] An earlier draft of this essay was delivered as one of a series of lectures on "The Philosophy
of Socrates" at the University of St. Andrews in the Winter and Spring Terms of 1981. Duly
revised, it appeared under the title "The Socratic Elenchus," in *Oxford Studies in Ancient
Philosophy* I (1983), 27–58 and 71–4.
[2] On the chronological order of Plato's dialogues see additional note 1.1.
[3] "Our customary method" (*R*. x, 596A5–7). This is the method of "investigating from a
hypothesis" (ἐξ ὑποθέσεως σκοπεῖσθαι) borrowed from the mathematicians (*Meno* 86E–87B)
– a hypothesis whose standard content for Plato, in the middle dialogues, is the existence of
(Platonic) Forms (*Phaedo* 99D4–100B7), thus predicating the search for "What the *F* is" on
the epistemological implications of this grand metaphysical "hypothesis": see *Socrates*, 63–4,
beginning with the comment on texts quoted there as T10, T11, T12, T13.
[4] *R*. IV, 435D, where the "method" followed in the tripartite analysis of the structure of the
soul is said to be a makeshift for the "longer route" which would have been ideally desirable
(investigation of the Form of the soul).
[5] μέθοδος, used often in dialogues of the middle and later periods, is a new word, created by
Plato in his middle period: its first occurrences in preserved Greek are in the *Phaedo* (79E3,
97B6). Since in his earlier and middle dialogues Plato writes pure Greek, seldom indulging
in idiolect, this neologism is itself an expression of his newfound interest in method. It is an
important terminological coinage, strangely overlooked in Lewis Campbell's discussion of
Plato's "technicalities" (1867: xxiv ff.).

no name for it. ἔλεγχος and the parent verb ἐλέγχειν ("to refute," "to examine critically," "to censure"),[6] he uses to describe,[7] not to baptize, what he does. Only in modern times[8] has *elenchus* become a proper name. The "What is the *F*?" question which Socrates pursues elenctically about other things he never poses about the elenchus, leaving us only his practice to guide us when we try to answer it for ourselves. Lacking his definition of it, ours can only be a hypothesis – a guess. And we may guess wrong.

I guessed wrong thirty-five years ago in the account of the elenchus I put into my Introduction to *Plato's Protagoras*[9] and so have others before or since. Here is the account in the article on "Dialectic" by Roland Hall in *The Encyclopedia of Philosophy* (1967):

> The Socratic elenchus was perhaps a refined form of the Zenonian paradoxes, a prolonged cross-examination which refutes the opponent's original thesis by getting him to draw from it, by means of a series of questions and answers, a consequence that contradicts it.

This comes close, but still not close enough. Obviously wrong is the suggestion that Socrates gets the opponent "to draw" that consequence. It is Socrates who draws it; the opponent has to be carried to it kicking and screaming. More objectionable is the assimilation of the elenchus to Zeno's dialectic, from which it differs in a fundamental respect. The refutands in Zeno's paradoxes are unasserted counterfactuals:

If there are many things, they must be both infinitely many and
    finitely many.
If there is motion, then the swiftest cannot overtake the slowest:
    Achilles will never catch up with the tortoise.

---

[6] The reader should bear in mind that the same terms are used by Plato in the middle dialogues (as e.g. at *R.* VII, 534C1–3) to refer to his own method, which is as different from that of Socrates as is the Platonic Form from the Socratic form, satisfying radically different categorial criteria (detailed in *Socrates*, ch. 2, section III). Throughout this essay I shall use "elenchus" *exclusively* as an abbreviation for "the Socratic elenchus."

[7] And this in great profusion. Dozens of uses of the noun and the verb in Plato, a majority of them in the earlier dialogues, as a look at Brandwood's *Word Index* (1976) will show.

[8] Perhaps no earlier than in George Grote, 1865, and Lewis Campbell, 1867, and then again in Henry Sidgwick, 1872, no doubt under the influence of Grote and Campbell, to whose work he refers.

[9] Vlastos, 1956. As I indicated in the Introduction to *Socrates*, I have revised some of the views I express there. Its most serious error is its misinterpretation of the elenchus and, consequently, of Socrates' profession of ignorance.

Socrates, on the other hand, as we shall see, will not debate un-asserted premises – only those asserted categorically by his interlocutor, who is not allowed to answer "contrary to his real opinion."

A third mistake is the suggestion that the consequence which contradicts the thesis is drawn *from* that thesis. This notion is an invention of Richard Robinson. He had maintained that Plato "habitually thought and wrote *as if* all elenchus consisted in reducing the thesis to a self-contradiction."[10] If that were true, Socrates' procedure would have been as follows: when the answerer asserts *p*, Socrates would derive *not-p* either directly from *p* or else by deriving from *p* further premises which entail *not-p* – in either case deducing the negation of *p* from *p* "without the aid of extra premisses."[11] The trouble with this picture is that what it pictures is not in our texts.[12] There are some 39 elenctic arguments by Robinson's count (*op. cit.*, 24) in Plato's earlier dialogues. Not one of them exhibits the pattern. The premises from which Socrates derives *not-p* generally do not include *p* and even when they do, there are others in the premise-set elicited from the interlocutor, not deducible from *p*.

If Socrates had thought he proved what, according to Robinson, Plato "habitually wrote and thought" as if he did, Socrates would have believed he was producing the strongest possible proof of the falsehood of *p*: there can be no stronger proof of the falsehood of a thesis than to show that it entails its own negation. What Socrates in fact does in any given elenchus is to convict *p* of being a member of an inconsistent premise-set; and to do this is not to show that *p* is false but only that either *p* is false or that some or all of the premises are false. The question then becomes how Socrates can claim, as I shall be arguing he does claim in "standard elenchus,"[13] to have proved that the refutand is false, when all he has established is its inconsistency with premises whose truth he has not tried to establish in that argument: they have entered the argument simply as propositions on which he and the interlocutor are agreed. This is *the*

---

[10] Robinson, 1953: 28. In spite of this and other mistakes, this is an admirable book. It served me as a model in my earlier Platonic studies. See the tribute to it in my review of Cherniss' *Collected Papers* (Vlastos, 1978: 538), and in *Socrates*, Introduction, n. 55.

[11] Robinson, *loc. cit.*

[12] As pointed out by Friedländer and Cherniss at the time: for the references see my review of Cherniss cited in n. 10.

[13] This term will be explained in section III below.

problem of the Socratic elenchus and it is spirited away in the account given by Robinson and repeated in *The Encyclopedia of Philosophy*.[14] I shall be returning to this problem in due course in the present chapter.

Let me then suggest a more defensible description:

Socratic elenchus is a search for moral truth by question-and-answer adversary argument in which a thesis is debated only if asserted as the answerer's own belief and is regarded as refuted only if its negation is deduced[15] from his own beliefs.

First and foremost elenchus is *search*. The adversary procedure which is suggested (but not entailed) by the Greek word (which *may* be used to mean "refutation," but may also be used to mean "testing" or, still more broadly, "censure," "reproach") is not an end in itself. If it were, Socrates' dialectic as depicted in Plato's earlier dialogues would be a form of eristic,[16] which it is not, because its object is always that positive outreach for truth which is expressed by words for searching (ἐρευνῶ, διερευνῶ), inquiring (ζητῶ, ἐρωτῶ, συνερωτῶ), investigating (σκοπῶ, διασκοπῶ, σκέπτομαι, διασκέπτομαι). This is what philosophy *is* for Socrates. When he thinks of being silenced by the authorities, he imagines them saying to him,

T1 *Ap*. 29c: "You shall no longer engage in this search nor philosophize,"

where the "nor" is epexegetic. Equivalently, for Socrates, to philosophize is to "examine" – he searches by "examining."

T2 *Ap*. 28e: "The god has commanded me ... to live philosophizing, examining myself and others."

Were he to go to Hades, he would go on

T3 *Ap*. 41b: "examining and searching there as I have been doing with people here."

---

[14] Kidd, 1967. It is still being repeated: "One of the commonest forms [of elenchus] is to argue that a given statement leads to a self-contradiction, in other words to two statements which are mutually contradictory" (Kerferd, 1981: 65, with a footnote citing Robinson as authority).

[15] The intended force of the argument is deductive throughout; resort to *epagoge* (which is frequent) is no exception, for *epagoge* is not true induction, though often mistaken for it: see Robinson, *op. cit.*, ch. 4, *Epagoge*; and Vlastos, *Socrates*, additional note 3.2, "Epagogic arguments."

[16] Cf. Socrates' description of "eristic *sophia*" in n. 29 below. And see additional note 1.2, "Elenchus versus eristic," below.

What is he searching for? For truth, certainly, but not for every sort of truth – only for truth in the moral domain. If we wanted to know what is the wholesale price of olive-oil on the Peiraeus market, Socrates would not propose that elenctic argument is the way to find out. Nor yet for, say,

(1)   What is the right diet for a patient with a fever?
(2)   What is the side of a square whose area is twice that of a given square?
(3)   What conditions must be satisfied by a true answer to a "What is the *F*?" question?

There is no reason to suppose that Socrates thinks that truths in the domain of the productive crafts or of mathematics or of logic are to be ascertained by elenctic argument. He never says or implies anything of the kind. Examples (2) and (3) are meant to be provocative. The mathematical one, of course, is from the interrogation of the slave-boy in the *Meno*. In the Socrates of this passage Plato has already taken a giant step – the doctrine of "recollection" – in transforming the moralist of the earlier dialogues into the metaphysician of the middle ones. The interrogation is laid on to support that doctrine – to help Meno "recollect" it (81c–82a). Elenchus is used in this passage to correct mistakes[17] – its proper, purely negative, use in philosophical dialectic in Plato's middle dialogues[18] – but not to discover, still less prove, the proposition which constitutes the true solution to the problem.[19]

---

[17] See my discussion of this point in *Socrates*, ch. 4, n. 54.
[18] *Phd.* 85c.
[19] The method of discovery in the interrogation of the slave-boy is *not* elenctic but maieutic, though the midwife metaphor is not used here, as it is not in any dialogue prior to the *Theaetetus*. Socrates sees the boy as getting the answer "not by learning it from me" (82b), but by "himself recovering knowledge from himself" (85d), which is what Socrates says of his interlocutors in the *Tht.*: "they have learned nothing from me but have themselves discovered for themselves" the sought-for truth (150d6–7). I agree with Burnyeat, 1977a, that the midwife metaphor is a Platonic invention: his argument for this thesis I find conclusive. I also agree that midwifery and recollection are distinct metaphors which should not be conflated. Even so, they have in common the fundamental notion, expressed in each of the two texts I have cited, that the true propositions discovered in the interrogation *do not come from Socrates* but from the interlocutor ("recollected" by him in the *Meno*, "brought forth" by him in the *Tht.*) – a notion which is not expressed in any of the earlier dialogues.

As to example (3), this does refer to the unreconstructed Socrates of the earlier dialogues.[20] But note that he does not elicit from his interlocutors, and does not debate, the logical conditions for the right answer to a "What is the *F*?" question: he produces these entirely on his own initiative, tells the interlocutors what they are, and requires them to comply, never inviting elenctic argument on whether or not they are the right conditions. Thus, when he tells Laches that the definition of "courage" must cover all the agreed-upon cases of courageous conduct, he does not ask, "Do you agree?" but only "Do you understand?"[21] And this is generally true. The interlocutor is never shown as having dissenting views about the logical pattern to which a proper definition must conform – views which need to be refuted by elenctic argument before the search can begin. He is shown as all at sea on the topic, needing instruction on its very rudiments, which Socrates is only too willing to provide. He offers it encountering not opposition but incomprehension.[22] The logical truths governing definition and the still more abstract ones, like the principle of non-contradiction,[23] are never treated as elenctic theses.[24] Only moral truths are so treated.

For "moral" Socrates has no special word.[25] But neither does he

---

[20] *La.* 191C–192B; *Eu.* 5D, 6D–E, 11A6–B1; *HMa.* 287Cff; *M.* 72A6ff. (Though this last passage occurs in a transitional dialogue, its place in that dialogue antecedes the introduction of the theory of recollection; paralleling closely the specifications which a correct definition must meet in the *Eu.* – cf. *M.* 72C6–D1 with *Eu.* 6D9–E6 – *M.* 72A6ff. is, clearly, a faithful reproduction of the definitional doctrine of the earlier dialogues.)

[21] 191E11: ἢ οὔπω καταμανθάνεις ὃ λέγω; Same question in *M.* 72D1: ἢ οὐ μανθάνεις ὅτι λέγω;

[22] Thus when Hippias says "there is no difference" between (a) "What is the beautiful?" and (b) "What is beautiful?" he is not represented as propounding an erroneous view which calls for refutation, but as exhibiting pitiful incapacity to understand the very meaning of those questions. Choosing to ignore Hippias' statement that there is no difference between (a) and (b), Socrates insists that it is (a) that should be answered (*HMa.* 287D–E).

[23] Thus when the interlocutors run into contradiction Socrates never feels that he has to argue that they have suffered logical disaster. The principle of non-contradiction is never so much as stated in the earlier dialogues (as it is in the middle ones: *R.* IV, 436E–437A), to say nothing of its being defended or justified.

[24] For the view that the conditions of a successful definition are not themselves subject to elenctic argument I am indebted directly to Paul Woodruff. See his remarks on the dependence of "definition-testing arguments" on "key premises supplied by Socrates" which "govern the form and content a definition must have to be acceptable"; on this matter Socrates acts as "an authority" (1982: 137–8).

[25] But in expounding Socratic doctrine he uses ἀρετή to mean "moral virtue": see my discussion of this important point in the opening paragraph of ch. 8 in *Socrates*.

have any difficulty indicating that what he is searching for is truth in the moral domain:

T4 *R.* I, 352D: "Our argument is over no chance matter but over *what is the way we ought to live.*" (The same phrase in identical words in *G.* 500C 3–4.)

T5 *G.* 487E–488A: "Of all investigations, Callicles, this is the noblest – about those things on which you reproached me: *what sort of man should one be, and what should one practice* and up to what point, when he is young and when he is old."

T6 *G.* 472C–D: "For the things we are disputing are hardly trivial but, as one might say, those which to come to know is noblest and not to know most base. For their sum and substance is just this: knowing, or not knowing, *who is happy and who is not.*"

These are the questions Socrates attacks by the elenctic method, and he treats them as never having been investigated heretofore by the right method, so that what the wise men of the past have or haven't said about them becomes of little consequence. When he is talking with you he wants to know your answer. If you quote some wise man's answer – as Polemarchus does in *Republic* 1 – he will discuss it as your answer, expecting you to defend it as yours. That you do not yourself have high credentials will not trouble him. He may even count it an advantage. As a partner in the search he welcomes

T7 *Ap.* 29D: " ... any one of you I happen to meet at any given time ... "

T8 *Ap.* 30A: " ... anyone, young or old, citizen or foreigner ... "

His is the aggressive outreach, the indiscriminate address to all and sundry, of the street evangelist. If you speak Greek and are willing to talk and reason, you can be Socrates' partner in searching, with the prospect that truth undisclosed to countless ages might be discovered here and now, on this spot, in the next forty minutes, between the two of you.

For success in this enterprise two constraints must be observed. The first is to refrain from speechifying – to give short, spare, direct, unevasive answers to the questions put to you. In a cooperative endeavor for mutual enlightenment this is self-explanatory. Not so the second – the "say what you believe" requirement:

T9 *G.* 500B: "By the god of friendship, Callicles, don't think that you can play games with me and answer whatever comes to your head, contrary to your real opinion (παρὰ τὰ δοκοῦντα)."[26]

T10 *R.* I, 346A: "My good man, don't answer contrary to your real opinion, so we may get somewhere."

T11 *Cr.* 49C–D: "If you agree with these things, Crito, watch out lest you are doing so contrary to your real opinion . . ."

To Protagoras, who had just said in reply to Socrates' question, "But what does it matter? Let it be so for us (ἔστω ἡμῖν), if you wish," Socrates says:

T12 *Pr.* 331C: "I won't have this. For it isn't this 'if you wish' and 'if you think so' that I want to be refuted, but you and me. I say 'you and me' for I think that the thesis is best refuted if you take the 'if' out of it."

Why should Socrates object to iffy theses? Hypothetical premises had always been legitimate not only in disputation, but even in the most stringent of all forms of argument as yet discovered in Greece: mathematical proof. It is standard in Greek geometry, where indirect proofs[27] employ an unasserted premise, prefaced by the word Protagoras had just used: ἔστω, "let this be so." Zeno, whose dialectic had become classical by this time – Aristotle calls him "the inventor of dialectic"[28] – had practiced systematically the thing Socrates forbids: each of his paradoxes investigates the contradictory consequences of its counterfactual premise. Why should Socrates ban this modality of philosophical argument? He doesn't say. I suggest that he has three reasons.

First, to test honesty in argument. In eristic, where the prime object is to win,[29] one is free to say anything that will give one a debating advantage. In elenchus, where the prime object is search

---

[26] Cf. also what he had said to Callicles earlier at 495A, and also what he says to the sophist at *Eud.* 286D: "Dionysodorus, are you saying this for the sake of talking – to say something outrageous – or do you really believe that no human being is ignorant?"

[27] E.g. Euclid, *Elements* I. 14.

[28] D.L. 9.25 and 29.

[29] Cf. the description of eristic *sophia*: "prowess in verbal contest and in the refutation of whatever is said, regardless of whether it is false or true" (*Eud.* 272A–B).

for truth, one does not have that option. One must say what one believes, even if it will lose one the debate.[30]

Second, to test one's seriousness in the pursuit of truth.[31] Seriousness can be feigned. One can put on a solemn face, a grave voice, shamming an earnestness one does not feel. But if one puts oneself on record as saying what one believes, one has given one's opinion the weight of one's life. Since people consider their opinions more expendable than their life, Socrates wants them to tie their opinions to their life as a pledge that what they say is what they mean.

A further reason comes from that other dimension of the elenchus to which I have made no allusion so far. It is highlighted in the *Apology* where Socrates' "search" is, at the same time, a challenge to his fellows to change their life, to cease caring for money and reputation and not caring for the most precious thing of all – what one is:

T13 *Ap.* 29E–30A: "And if one of you says ... he does care, I will not let him go nor leave him, but will question and examine and refute him. And if he seems to me not to have the virtue he says he has, I shall reproach him for undervaluing the things of greatest value and overvaluing trivial ones."

Socrates is not always so inquisitorial and censorious. But those who know him best understand that the elenchus does have this existential dimension – that what it examines is not just propositions but lives. Says Nicias, an old acquaintance of Socrates, to Lysimachus, a new one:

T14 *La.* 187E–188A: "I don't think you realize that he who comes closest to Socrates in discussion, even if he should start discussing something else, will not cease being carried round and round in argument until he falls into giving an account of his own self – of the way he lives now and has lived in the past. And when he does, Socrates will not let him go until he has done a thorough job of sifting him."

---

[30] Socrates says to Gorgias "I am one of those who would gladly be refuted if what I say is not true," adding that if Gorgias does not share that sentiment further debate would be pointless (458A–B).

[31] Note the connection Socrates sees between "saying what you believe" and seriousness in argument at T9 above, which continues: "Nor must you think of me as playing games. For you see what the argument is all about – and is there anything about which even a man of little sense could be more serious than this: what is the way we ought to live?" (*G.* 500B–C; cf. T4 above). The same connection of the rule with seriousness in argument is made at *R.* I, 349A, and is implied in the question to Dionysodorus quoted in n. 26 above.

Thus elenchus has a double objective: to discover how every human being ought to live *and* to test that single human being who is doing the answering – to find out if *he* is living as one ought to live. This is a two-in-one operation. Socrates does not provide for two types of elenchus – a philosophical one, searching for truth about the good life, and a therapeutic one, searching out the answerer's own in the hope of bringing him to the truth. There is one elenchus and it must do both jobs, though one or the other will be to the fore in different phases of it. From this point of view, too, the "say what you believe" requirement makes sense. How could Socrates hope to get you to give, sooner or later, an account of your life, if he did not require you to state your personal opinion on the questions under debate?

This will also explain why on some occasions Socrates is willing to waive the rule. So, for example, when the interlocutor is losing the debate, sees disaster ahead, and tries to spare his battered ego further mauling by shifting from combatant to bystander. This happens to Protagoras shortly after the passage quoted as T12 above. By this time he has lost two arguments. At the start of the third this exchange occurs:

T15 *Pr.* 333B–C: S.: "Do you believe that one who acts unjustly may act temperately in so doing?"[32] Pr.: "Socrates, I would be ashamed to agree to that. But many would agree." S.: "Shall I address my argument to them or to you?" Pr.: "Argue first against that view of the many, if you wish." S.: "It makes no difference to me, provided you do the answering. For what I chiefly examine is the proposition. But the consequence may be that I the questioner and you the answerer will also be examined."

When Protagoras was looking for the same kind of shelter earlier on by hedging his answer with "if you wish," Socrates had blocked the move, indicating that Protagoras had already taken a stand and would be held to it: his ego was already on the line, as in elenchus it must be, for otherwise Socrates would be left with a proposition detached from a person willing to predicate his life on it, and this Socrates would refuse, as in fact he did refuse at the time. Once that is settled, Socrates is willing to make concessions, as a *pis aller* and under protest, so that the argument may go on: Protagoras is allowed

---

[32] ἆρα τίς σοι δοκεῖ ἀδικῶν ἄνθρωπος σωφρονεῖν, ὅτι ἀδικεῖ;

to save face by handing over his part to that faceless surrogate, "the many." For the same reason Socrates lets this happen again, and on a bigger scale, later in the dialogue, where he directs his argument for the impossibility of *akrasia* to the same notional answerer, "the many," dragging along Protagoras as a make-believe ally (352Eff.). At the end of that debate we see that Socrates takes the consequence to be that, given Protagoras' subsequent admissions (crucially the ones at 358 A5-6, B3-5), he has been "examined" after all, compelled to confess that *his* thesis – not just that of "the many" – has been shown to be "impossible" (360E).

II

Because it is allowed the waywardness of impromptu debate, elenctic argument may take any number of different routes. But through its motley variations the following pattern, which I shall call "standard elenchus," is preserved:

(1)   The interlocutor asserts a thesis, *p*, which Socrates considers false and targets for refutation.

(2)   Socrates secures agreement to further premises, say *q* and *r* (each of which may stand for a conjunct of propositions).[33] The agreement is *ad hoc*: Socrates argues from $\{q, r\}$, not to them.

(3)   Socrates then argues, and the interlocutor agrees, that *q & r* entail *not-p*.

(4)   Socrates then claims that he has shown that *not-p* is true, *p* false.

Here are some of the theses Socrates establishes in this way (the list is not meant to be exhaustive):

that the poet versifies and the rhapsode recites not by craft, but by a kind of madness (*Ion*);

that in matters of justice we should follow not "the many" but "the man who knows" (*Cr.* 47A–48A);

that we should never return wrong for wrong or evil for evil (*Cr.* 48B–49C);

---

[33] I use two variables, though one would suffice, with a view to the special case, to be discussed in section III below, where the interlocutor has the option of welshing on just one of the agreed-upon premises.

that piety and justice, temperance and wisdom, are interentailing
   (*Pr.* 329E–333B);

that pious action is god-loved because it is pious, not pious because
   it is god-loved (*Eu.* 9D–11A);

that the just man will not harm his enemies (*R.* I, 335);

that the just ruler rules not for his own benefit but for that of his
   subjects (*R.* I, 338C–347D);

that to teach men justice is *ipso facto* to make them just (*G.* 460A–C);

that the good is not the pleasant and the pleasant is not the good and
   that pleasure should be pursued for the sake of the good, not
   vice versa (*G.* 494E–500A);

that it is better to suffer wrong than to commit it and to suffer
   deserved punishment than to escape it (the great argument in
   the *Gorgias*, made first against Polus and then, with different
   premises, against Callicles).

The main alternative to this pattern is, in Robinson's terminology,[34] "indirect elenchus." I believe that Robinson overestimates its
frequency relative to that of "direct elenchus,"[35] and I propose to
concentrate now on standard elenchus, which I regard as Socrates'
main instrument of research, as shown by the positive theses he
establishes by this form of argument. My discussion will focus on
points (2) and (4), for this is how I can best set in historiographic

---

[34] *Op. cit.* 22ff. In "indirect elenchus" the falsehood of *p* is demonstrated by assuming its truth
alongside that of *q* and *r* and arguing that, since the premise-set $\{p, q, r\}$ is inconsistent
and the interlocutor stands by the truth of *q & r*, he must infer that *p* is false. So in point of
logic there is no substantial difference from standard elenchus. As Polansky suggested
(1985: n. 3) my treatment of indirect elenchus was wrongly dismissive of it in the 1983 version of this paper. (I am accepting Polansky's point that at *R.* I, 349D "indirect elenchus"
is used.)

[35] He counts 31 indirect elenchi in nine dialogues (p. 24). But it is hard to know what to make
of this figure because he does not give the references from which it could be checked. In any
case he fails to recognize how many of Socrates positive doctrines are established by
standard elenchus and how different is the relative weight placed on it. Thus in the
argument against Polemarchus (*R.* I, 331Eff.) indirect elenchus is used to rough him up
(333D, 334A–B) without reaching any positive result, merely discrediting the ultra-respect-
able definition Polemarchus defends, keeping standard elenchus in reserve until it is needed
to establish the powerful Socratic thesis that the just man will not harm his enemies
(335B–C). Similarly, Euthyphro's first definition is attacked by indirect elenchus (6E–
8A) and standard elenchus is then brought in to prove the doctrine, so fundamental for
Socrates' rational theology, that pious action is god-loved *because* it is pious, not vice versa
(9D–11A).

perspective the interpretation of the elenchus I am defending here. At those two points I am departing sharply from each of the leading lines of past interpretation, represented respectively in two works of nineteenth-century scholarship which are landmark studies in the field: Zeller, *Philosophie der Griechen*,[36] George Grote, *Plato and the Other Companions of Sokrates*.[37] I am going against Zeller at point (2), against Grote at point (4). Since Grote's Socrates is incomparably more interesting than Zeller's and, in my view, much closer to the truth, I shall have more to say of the relation of my Socrates to Grote's than to Zeller's.

The claim I am making at point (2) is that the premises $\{q, r\}$ from which Socrates deduces the negation of the opponent's thesis in any given argument are logically unsecured within that argument. He asks the interlocutor if he agrees, and if he gets agreement he goes on from there. So in elenctic argument there is no appeal to what Aristotle takes to be the court of last resort for settling philosophical disagreements: none, on one hand, to those self-certifying truths which are for Aristotle the foundation of all demonstrative argument;[38] and none, on the other, to what he calls τὰ ἔνδοξα – propositions worthy of belief because they are believed "by all or by most or by the wise and, of these, by all or most or the most distinguished and most reputable" (*Top.* 100a29–b23), which constitute for Aristotle the foundation of "dialectical argument" – the form of argument proper to moral inquiry. Socrates makes no appeal to either. He never tells the interlocutor that he must grant a premise because it is a self-certifying truth nor yet because it is the most reputable of the opinions on the topic. To self-evidence there is no appeal at all by anyone in Plato's earlier dialogues.[39] To common belief there is,

---

[36] The volume entitled *Sokrates und die Sokratiker*. My reference will be to the English translation of the third German edition by Reichel, 1885.

[37] Cited previously in n. 8.

[38] Demonstration (ἀπόδειξις) proceeds from premises which are "primary" (πρῶτα), i.e. "induce conviction through themselves and not through other things (μὴ δι' ἑτέρων ἀλλὰ δι' αὑτῶν ἔχοντα τὴν πίστιν)" (*Top.* 100a27–b19; cf. *Pr. An.* 64b34ff.; *Phys.* 193a4–6).

[39] Contrary to what is sometimes implied in the scholarly literature – most recently by Reeve, 1989: 165, who describes elenchus as "the practice of refuting propositions by showing them to have entailments inconsistent with obvious truths." Gulley, 1968: 43–4, holds that in elenchus Socrates aims "to establish as the contradictory of the respondent's initial thesis a proposition presented as so obviously true that the respondent is driven to abandon his

but not by Socrates. It is Polus who appeals to it in the *Gorgias*, only
to find Socrates rejecting the appeal out of hand.

T16 *G.* 473E: "Socrates, don't you think you've been refuted already when
you say things with which no one would agree? Just ask any of these people
here."

Socrates stands on his repeatedly expressed conviction that the
only opinion which matters in the argument is that of the arguers
themselves:

T17 *G.* 472B–C (and cf. 474A–B):   "If I cannot produce one man – yourself –
to witness to my assertions, I believe that I shall have accomplished nothing ...
Neither will you, I believe, if this one man – myself – does not witness for you,
letting all those other people go."[40]

At this point the Socrates of Plato's earlier dialogues is at logger-
heads with Xenophon's:

T18 *Mem.* 4.6.15:   Whenever Socrates himself argued something out he proceeded from the most strongly held opinions,[41] believing that security in argument lies therein. Accordingly, whenever he argued he got much greater assent
from his hearers than anyone I have ever known.

That *Xenophon's* Socrates got much greater assent from his hearers
than anyone Xenophon has ever known is no doubt true, but tells us
nothing about the real Socrates. For when we compare Xenophon's
Socrates with Plato's we find the former sadly reduced, shorn of those
doctrines which, as I have argued in *Socrates*, constitute the latter's
most distinctive innovations. Thus that the performance of ritualis-
tic acts is not an essential component of piety, whose core must be
ethical, for it is interentailing with the other virtues, beginning with
justice, is not in Xenophon, where conformity to the "usages" of

---

thesis." This is surely false. Thus in the *G.* in each of Socrates' arguments against Gorgias,
Polus, and Callicles the contradictory of their thesis is a paradox – not at all likely to strike
the sponsor of the refutand as "obviously true," no matter how it is presented to him. Thus
in the second argument against Polus the contradictory of Polus' thesis is that it is better to
suffer injustice than to commit it and better to submit to deserved punishment than to
escape it; after Socrates has "proved" this (*G.* 479E8), its immediate consequences continue
to strike Polus as "outrageous" (ἄτοπα, 480E1).

[40] For Socrates' rejection of the appeal to common opinion see also *La.* 184E, *Cr.* 46D–47D.

[41] διὰ τῶν μάλιστα ὁμολογουμένων. There is no completely satisfactory translation of this
phrase. But I would agree with Donald Morrison, 1987: 15, that my previous rendering of
it as "the most generally accepted opinions" is too weak, the literal meaning being "the
things above all assented to," μάλιστα conveying "intensity as well as frequency."

cult is made definitive of piety[42] and Socrates is represented as rebutting the charge of impiety by alleging that he was "most visible of all men" in cult-service to the gods of the state (*Mem.* 1.2.64).[43] The rejection of retaliation and of the age-old view that it is as just to do evil to enemies as to do good to friends, is not in Xenophon, whose Socrates, on the contrary, firmly declares for the traditional sentiment.[44]

Are we to say that whenever Socrates vindicates such novelties against determined opponents he succeeds in producing conviction? Not if we listen to Plato instead of Xenophon. The theses which have been "proved" (*G.* 479E8) against Polus still strike him as "outrageous" (ἄτοπα, *G.* 480E1). Such seems to be the state of mind in which Socrates leaves his opponents repeatedly in Plato. Trounced in debate, seeing no prospect of faring better if they were to renew the argument, Gorgias and Callicles in the *Gorgias* (460E, 510A), Protagoras in the *Protagoras* (361D), Thrasymachus in *Republic* I (354A), Euthyphro in the *Euthyphro* (14A–E) give no indication of having had a change of heart on the disputed point. There is no good reason to believe that Socrates would have won greater assent in Xenophon if he had argued for the same theses, as in fact he does not: in Xenophon ethical conduct does not displace ritual observance at the center of piety; there is no interdiction of returning evil for evil, and the relation of virtue to happiness and of knowledge to virtue is blurred and flattened out – the paradoxes become commonplaces.

In saying this, I am not restricting in the least Socrates' freedom to use commonly accepted beliefs among the agreed-upon premises from which he deduces the negation of the opponent's thesis. *Any* proposition on whose truth he and the interlocutor agree is grist to his mill. If the proposition is a "reputable belief" or an "obvious truth," so much the better. The point on which Plato's Socrates, unlike Xenophon's, could not agree with Aristotle is the *principle*

---

[42] The "pious man" is defined as he who honours the gods in conformity to the customary usages (τὰ νόμιμα, *Mem.* 4.6.4).

[43] Cf. *Socrates*, additional note 6.4, "Xenophon on sacrifice."

[44] Cf. *Socrates*, ch. 7, "Socrates' rejection of retaliation" and additional note 7.1, "Plato vs. Xenophon on Socrates' rejection of retaliation."

that "reputable beliefs" constitute the court of last appeal for settling moral disagreement.[45] For so bold an innovator in ethics to
concede this principle to his opponents would have been disastrous.
It would have offered them a short way of refuting those of his
ethical views which went flat against traditional moral sentiment.
No belief would count as more reputable in current opinion – and
would continue to hold this status for centuries to come in Greco-
Roman antiquity – than the one which puts doing evil to enemies on
a par with doing good to friends and sanctifies retaliation as a
principle of justice. Those Socratic views which strike Callicles as
"turning our human life upside down" (*G.* 481c) would not have
had a leg to stand on if appeal to what Aristotle calls "reputable
beliefs" and Xenophon "most strongly held opinions" were accepted
as foundational in moral inquiry.

So the conflict between Plato's testimony and Xenophon's is un-
negotiable, and the gravest fault in Zeller, great historian though
he was, is that he sided with Xenophon's instead of Plato's account of this fundamental matter. Declaring that "the peculiarity"
of Socrates' method was "deducing conceptions from the common
opinions of men,"[46] Zeller misses completely what Plato recognizes
as the peculiarity of Socrates' method: getting results not by appealing "to the common opinions of men" but by deducing the
refutans of the interlocutors' theses *from their own beliefs*.[47] Zeller
thereby bequeathed to the historians who followed him – most recently Guthrie[48] – an account of Socrates' method of argument
which is fatal to the elenchus. And so we see in Zeller,[49] and now

---

[45] In 1983: 43, n. 41 I claimed that Socrates requires some non-endoxic premises to reach
contra-endoxic conclusions. Various critics have objected (Kraut, 1983; Polansky, 1985;
Morrison, 1987). They have given me good reason to renounce my former claim, but none
to convince me of its contrary. So far as I can see now, the point is undecidable on the
textual evidence and anyhow, my former claim is dispensable: I have dispensed with
it entirely in expounding the Socratic view in the text above.

[46] *Op. cit.* 121, citing (at 122, n. 1) *Mem.* 4.6.15 (cited above as T18).

[47] And Zeller fails to recognize that on this point Aristotle implicitly supports Plato against
Xenophon, since for Aristotle the reason why Socrates "asked questions, but did not answer
them" is that "he confessed he had no knowledge" (*Soph. El.* 183b7–8): one who professes
to have no knowledge and cannot argue ὡς εἰδώς (*ibid.* b3) would have no option but employ what Aristotle calls "peirastic" argument in which one argues "from the answerer's
own beliefs" (ἐκ τῶν δοκούντων τῷ ἀποκρινομένῳ, *ibid.* 165b4–5).

[48] Guthrie, 1969 and 1975.

[49] No discussion of the elenchus in Zeller, *op. cit.* ch. 6 ("The philosophical method of Socrates"). None in Guthrie either (see next note).

again in Guthrie,[50] the elenchus disappear without a trace. It is not argued out of their account of Socrates' philosophical method. It just drops out.

III

Now for point (4) in my analysis of standard elenchus: the most novel of my proposals.[51] I must begin with the position I had reached in my earlier Socratic studies – the extreme opposite of the view I wish to defend now. Explicitly in that brief Introduction to the *Protagoras* (1956) to which I alluded above (n. 9), implicitly in the essay on the "Paradox of Socrates" (1958) written around the same time, I had maintained that Socrates never went beyond (3) in his elenctic arguments – that their object was simply to reveal to his interlocutors confusions and muddles within themselves, jarring their adherence to some confident dogma by bringing to their awareness its collision with other, no less confident, presumptions of theirs. This is Plato's later picture of "the sophist of noble lineage" in the *Sophist* (230A–E), whose service to his interlocutors is simply therapy ("purgation") by enhanced self-knowledge: their dogmatism is battered as they are made aware of conflicts within their own beliefs. It should be noted that nothing is said to make this "purgative" art a subdivision of eristic.[52] What we get in this retrospective view of

---

[50] Which is all the more surprising in that he, unlike Zeller, takes Plato to be "the chief, and Xenophon only an auxiliary, source of our knowledge of Socrates as a philosopher" (1969: 350).

[51] My interpretation of standard elenchus, taken as a whole, and applied rigorously, conceived as *the only final support* Socrates offers his moral doctrines, has no clear precedent in the scholarly literature, to my knowledge. Its affinities are with views like those of Gulley, 1968: 37ff., and Irwin, 1977: 37ff., and 1979, who also recognize that the elenchus has positive, no less than negative, thrust, aiming to give argumentative support to Socrates' affirmative views. My difference from Gulley was indicated in n. 39 above. As for Irwin, who does understand that in Plato, unlike Xenophon, "the elenchus was Socrates' method of securing agreement" (1974: 412), residual difference arises over his view (1977: 37) that "not all [of Socrates'] positive doctrines rely on the elenchus; some rely on the analogy between virtue and craft." I see no sound reason for putting this analogy outside the elenchus: all of the arguments which draw conclusions from that analogy are pure elenctic arguments. A further disagreement arises over alleged constraints which, according to Irwin, Socrates "normally" imposes on what the interlocutor can or can't say: "normally [the interlocutor] is not allowed this freedom [sc. to reject counter-examples which refute his proposed definition]" (1977: 39). On my understanding of the elenchus Socrates always allows – indeed requires – his interlocutors to say anything they believe, if they believe it (T9, T10, T11, T12 above).

[52] *Pace* Lewis Campbell (*op. cit.*, 191) and others: see Cornford, 1935: 177–82.

Socrates is an authentic, if partial, representation of Socrates.[53] This is the Socrates who destroys the "conceit of wisdom" (*Ap.* 21B–23B). But Plato never says this is all Socrates was, as he would have been, if the account of the elenchus I gave at that time were correct.

This interpretation had a mighty precedent in the work of that great Victorian student of Greek antiquity, whose multivolume *History of Greece* (1851) and three-volume *Plato* (1865) are, in my opinion, still, all in all, the finest contributions yet made in their respective themes. Unlike Zeller, Grote saw with the utmost clarity how central was the elenchus to Socratic inquiry as depicted in Plato's earlier dialogues, how central it had to remain in our picture of Socrates if we were to put any faith at all in Plato's testimony, and how valuable a contribution to human thought its relentless polemic against dogmatism would be, even if it were only the negative instrument Grote thought it.[54]

So while that picture of Socrates in my earlier work was very much of a minority view, it did not put me in bad company, and its foundation in Plato's depiction of elenctic argument in his earlier dialogues seemed secure: how could Plato be telling us, I used to ask myself, that his Socrates undertakes to prove that his interlocutors' theses were false and his own true, if all he shows Socrates doing is proving the inconsistency of his interlocutors' theses with other, unargued-for, concessions of theirs? But neither was that picture trouble-free. It left me with this question: if that were all Socrates expected to get from the elenchus – exposure of his interlocutors' inconsistencies – where did he find positive support for those strong doctrines of his on whose truth he based his life? If the elenchus, his only line of argument, gave those doctrines no rational grounding, what did? Grote had not been troubled by that question because he found it possible to believe that Socrates' own positive convictions and his critical assaults on those of others ran on separate tracks.[55] I

---

[53] The identification with Socrates is clinched in the back-reference to the passage in 268B–c: "we set him down as having no knowledge." So too in Alcibiades' speech in the *Symposium* we know that the subject of his tale is the Socrates of Plato's earlier dialogues when we see him described as "ignorant and knowing nothing" (216D).

[54] See especially 1865: I 236–77 and 281ff.; and his remarks on the elenchus in *A History of Greece*, part II, ch. 68 (vol. IX, p. 85 in the Everyman edn.).

[55] "The negative cross-examination, and the affirmative dogmatism, are ... two unconnected operations of thought: the one does not lead to, or involve, or verify, the other" (Grote, 1865: I 292).

could not. I could not reconcile myself to Grote's missionary of the examined life who was a dogmatist himself. And there were certainly textual grounds too for uneasiness with the picture, as critics started pointing out.[56] So I began to lose my enthusiasm for it. But it is one thing to become disgruntled with a picture, quite another to liberate oneself from it by discovering the textual evidence that destroys the picture. This I could not get from my critics, because they did not have it themselves. I had to discover it myself.

The crucial text[57] is

T19 *G.* 479E: "Has it not been proved (ἀποδέδεικται) that what was asserted [by myself] is true?"

Here Socrates says in so many words that he has done what Grote and I had maintained he never did in an elenctic argument: "proved" his thesis "true." Grote had certainly gone over that sentence many times, and so had I, and so had scores of others. But it had not hit anyone between the eyes.[58] Let us see what it means when read in its own context.

The argument starts half a dozen Stephanus pages back, where Socrates presses the question: if one were forced to choose between inflicting injustice on another person and suffering it oneself, which would be one's better choice? Polus takes the first option. His thesis is

p   To commit injustice is better than to suffer it.

Socrates defends what he takes to be the logical contradictory,

not-p   To suffer injustice is better than to commit it.

Attacking in standard elenctic fashion, he gets Polus to agree to a flock of further premises, only one of which need be recalled here:

q   To commit injustice is baser (αἴσχιον) than to suffer it,

while all the rest can be bundled up in a single gather-all conjunct

---

[56] The clearest and sharpest objection was raised by Dodds, 1959: 16 and n. 2. See also Gulley, *op. cit.*, 68ff.

[57] But by no means the only one. There are many others from which the same objection to Grote could be made (e.g., T17 above, and T20, T21 below). But this is the most striking and flat-footed one, leaving no room for cavil.

[58] There is no comment on it in Dodds' or Irwin's commentary and no reference to it in Gulley, though it should have been a star text for all three.

r, whose contents need not concern us.[59] Socrates argues, and Polus
agrees, that *q* and *r* entail *not-p*. On the strength of this result Socrates
feels empowered to tell Polus, in the words I just quoted, that his
own thesis, *not-p*, has been proved true.[60]

Why had Socrates' plain words in T19 been ignored? Why had I
ignored them myself? Because I had scaled them down, even while
reading them, discounting them as a careless overstatement. I would
not have done so if I had noticed that it is not only here, in the last
gasps of the debate with Polus, that Socrates says he can prove *not-p*
true: he makes the same claim in different words several pages back,
near the start of the debate. Recall what he had told Polus in T17
above: "If I cannot produce one man, yourself, to witness to my
assertions, I believe that I shall have accomplished nothing..."
Conceding that "almost all men, Athenians and foreigners, would
agree with you" (472A), he had declared,

T20 *G*. 472B: "But I, a single man, do not agree, for you do not compel me,
but produce a multitude of false witnesses against me, trying to drive me out
from my property, the truth (ἐκ τῆς οὐσίας καὶ τοῦ ἀληθοῦς)."

How do you "compel" your adversary to affirm what he denies?
In an argument your only means of compulsion are logical.[61] So to
"compel" Polus to "witness" for *not-p* Socrates would have to give
Polus *a logically compelling proof* that *p* is false. Thus already at 472B,
seven Stephanus pages before asserting, at T19 above, that he has
"proved" his thesis true, Socrates is announcing that this is exactly
what he is going to do. Thus *pace* Grote, ex-Vlastos, and who knows
how many others, there can be no question but that this long argument, elenchus in its standard form, which in point of logic has
done no more than demonstrate inconsistency within the premise-set

---

[59] For an analysis of the argument see *Socrates*, ch. 5, section III.

[60] Socrates' other two descriptions of the result (*G*. 479C4–7, 480B2–5) go no further than
pointing out the demonstrated inconsistency between Polus' thesis and the premises to
which he has agreed. But neither does he say anything to withdraw or weaken the claim he
makes in T19. (The reader should bear in mind that throughout this chapter I set aside all
questions relating to the logical validity of the reasoning by which Socrates undertakes to
refute his opponent's thesis in specific elenchi. For this whole aspect of Socratic dialectic I
may refer to Santas, 1979, with whose detailed analyses of Socratic arguments I find myself
in substantial agreement.)

[61] To coercion of this sort there can be, surely, no objection. If your opponent concedes the
truth of your premises and the validity of the inferences you draw from them, then, if he
wants to be rational, he has no option but to accept the conclusion.

$\{p, q, r\}$, Socrates takes to prove that p is false, *not-p* true. And in one of his asides we see him claiming that he can do the same against all comers:

T21 *G.* 474A5–6: "But I know how to produce one witness to my assertions: the man against whom I am arguing."

The claim he is making is perfectly general: whenever he is arguing elenctically against a thesis Socrates "knows" how to make the opponent "witness" to its contradictory, i.e. make him admit that the thesis is false. Conversely, he maintains that it is "impossible" for the opponent to do the same thing to him. When Polus taunts him, saying ironically it would be "more difficult" to refute the Socratic thesis, Socrates retorts,

T22 *G.* 473B10–11: "Not just difficult, Polus, but impossible: for what is true is never refuted."

This brings us smack up against what I had called earlier on "*the problem of the elenchus*": how is it that Socrates claims to have proved a thesis false when, in point of logic, all he has proved is that the thesis is inconsistent with the conjunction of agreed-upon premises for which no reason has been given in that argument? Could he be blind to the fact that logic does not warrant that claim? Let me frame the question in the terms of the metaphor that runs through the passage: compelling a witness to testify against himself. Suppose the following were to happen: a witness gives testimony p on his own initiative and then, under prodding from the prosecuting attorney, concedes q and r, whereupon the attorney points out to him that q and r entail *not-p*, and the witness agrees that they do. Has he then been compelled to testify that p is false? He has not. Confronted with the conflict in his testimony, it is still up to him to decide which of the conflicting statements he wants to retract. So Polus, if he had had his wits about him, might have retorted:

I see the inconsistency in what I have conceded, and I must do something to clean up the mess. But I don't have to do it your way. I don't have to concede that p is false. I have other options. For example, I could decide that p is true and q false. Nothing you have proved denies me this alternative.

And why shouldn't Polus in that crunch decide to throw q instead of p to the lions? How strongly he believes in p we have already seen:

he thinks it absurd of Socrates to deny it when almost all the world affirms it.[62] For *q*, on the other hand, he has no enthusiasm. He may have conceded it only, as Callicles observes later, "because he was ashamed to speak his mind" (*G.* 482E2). Why shouldn't Polus then jettison *q* with the feeling "good riddance"? He would then have come out of the elenchus believing that doing injustice is better and *nobler* than suffering it; his latter state would have been worse than his first. Couldn't this always happen? Whenever Socrates proved to his interlocutors that the premises they had conceded entailed the negation of their thesis, why couldn't they hang on to their thesis by welshing on one or more of the conceded premises?

Surely Socrates would be aware of this ever present possibility. Why then is he not worried by it? Because, I submit, he believes that if that wrong choice were made *he would have the resources to recoup that loss in a further elenchus.* This, I am suggesting, is his general view. If you disappointed him by denying *q* instead of *p*, he is confident that he could start all over again and find other premises inside your belief system to show you that you haven't got rid of the trouble – that if you keep *p*, it will go on making trouble for you, conflicting with these new premises as it did with *q* and *r* before. Can it be shown from the text that Socrates has this confidence? I want to argue that it can.

For a start let us observe what happens in the *Gorgias* after the argument against Polus is completed: Callicles is brought in to enact the role Polus might have played if he had chosen to retract *q* instead of *p*. Polus was worsted in the argument, says Callicles, only because he had conceded *q*, which he would not have done if he had been less squeamish. If he had had the fortitude to admit that to do injustice is nobler than to suffer it, he would have escaped unscathed (482D7–E2). Is this what happens? Not on your life. Socrates sheds no tears over the loss of *q*. He extracts a new premise-set from Callicles and, sure enough, this new set contains the premises he needs to deduce *not-p* all over again. But what if a super-Callicles should arise to repudiate these new premises from which Socrates derived *not-p*? Is there evidence that Socrates would not be fazed even then, or even by a super-super-Callicles after that? Does our

---

[62] Above T16.

text attest Socrates' belief that no flesh-and-blood antagonist will
ever turn up without always carrying along, in his own system of
belief, a baggage of premises from which he can be "compelled" to
"testify" against *p*? I want to argue that it does in two remarks
which, taken together, yield clear evidence that Socrates believes
this very thing.

The first is one of the things he says to Polus before their argument
begins:

T23 *G.* 474B: "I believe that I and you and the rest of mankind believe that
committing injustice is worse [for the agent] than is suffering it."

What in the world could Socrates mean by saying that Polus and
the multitudes who agree with him "believe" the opposite of what
they assert? There is only one way I see of making sense of that
remark: we must understand Socrates to be using "believe" in that
marginal sense of the word in which we may be all said to "believe"
innumerable things that have never entered our heads but are nonetheless *entailed* by what we believe in the common use of the word. I
shall call the latter "overt," the former "covert," belief.[63] Thus, if I
believe overtly that Mary is John's sister and that John is Bill's
grandfather, I may be said to believe covertly that Mary is Bill's
great-aunt, even if I never thought of that fact – indeed, even if I do
not have the word "great-aunt" in my vocabulary. Or, to take a
less trivial example, if I believe that a given figure is a Euclidean
triangle, then I believe covertly the proposition that was so surprising when we first learned it in geometry: that the figure's interior
angles sum to two right angles.

Here then is something Socrates might wish to express by saying
that Polus & Co. "believe" *not-p*, even while they insist that *p* is
what they do believe – namely, that they have certain beliefs of the
ordinary, overt, sort which entail *not-p*. This gives us a lucid sense for
what Socrates might be saying in our text. He is not declining to
take Polus & Co. at their word when they insist that *p* is what they
believe. Taking their word for this he is telling them that, along with
their (overt) belief in *p*, they have certain other (overt) beliefs which
entail *not-p*. In this sense they do (covertly) believe *not-p*.

---

[63] The terminology was suggested to me by David Gauthier. Alternatively, we might speak of
"explicit" and "tacit" belief.

Now consider what Socrates says to Callicles in the little speech that forms the curtain-raiser to their debate:

T24 *G.* 482A–B: [a] "Don't be astonished that I should say these things. My love, philosophy, is the one you must stop from asserting them. It is she, my friend, who asserts these things you hear from me, and she is much less unstable than is my other love. For the son of Cleinias [i.e. Alcibiades, Socrates' boy-love – 481D] says now one thing, now another, while philosophy always says the same thing. She says the things you find astonishing; you were yourself present when they were spoken."

[b] "So you must either refute her saying those very things that I was asserting – that to commit injustice and do so with impunity is the greatest of evils – or, if you leave this unrefuted, then, by the dog, god of Egypt, Callicles will not agree with you, Callicles, but will dissent from you your whole life long."

What could Socrates mean by telling Callicles that if he cannot refute the Socratic thesis then, in spite of his scornful rejection of it, it will remain in him as a source of lifelong internal dissension? How will it remain in him at all, if he repudiates it absolutely? Surely in the same way in which Polus was said in T23 to "believe" the thesis he repudiates: he will believe it (covertly) in virtue of believing (overtly) certain other things which, unbeknown to him, entail that thesis. Thus Callicles is being told that if he cannot refute the Socratic thesis (and he is not being encouraged to think that he can), he will *always* (his "whole life long") believe propositions which entail it.

Here we have conclusive evidence for Socrates' conviction that when he shows his interlocutors the inconsistency of their thesis with the conjunction of premises to which they have agreed, they will *never* succeed in saving their thesis by retracting one or more of the conceded premises; if they try to save it in that way, they are bound to fail; fail they must, if, regardless of which of them they retract, there will *always* be others in their belief system which entail the Socratic thesis.[64]

---

[64] A critic (Kraut, 1983: 65) says this would be "an astonishing claim for Socrates to make." True. Some of the claims Socrates makes *are* astonishing: see additional note 1.3 below. The critic objects that "Socrates would have realized that he had only a finite number of arguments for his conclusions." Quite so. Both Socrates and his opponent are finite creatures and sooner or later each of them will run out of steam. What Socrates is claiming is that his resources will always match those of his interlocutor. Anything impossible about that?

Socrates then is making a tremendous assumption. Stated in fullest generality, it comes to this:

[A]   Whoever has a false moral belief will always have at the same time true beliefs entailing the negation of that false belief.

That he is counting on the truth of this assumption is implied unambiguously if we presume – as we surely may – that what he says at T24 [b] he would also say about any of the theses he rebuts in elenctic arguments. We could also have derived this result, though not so directly, from T23. For this reveals Socrates' assurance that Polus *"and the rest of mankind"* who have the false belief p have nonetheless true beliefs entailing the negation of p: if Polus belongs to "mankind," he must have the beliefs entailing the negation of p. He cannot get out of his predicament by retracting q, for whatever other premise he may substitute for q will still leave him harboring beliefs which entail *not-p*. And this is what Socrates reveals more directly in his remark to Callicles at T24 [b]. What this shows, when fully generalized, is that anyone who clings to his false thesis will "always" his "whole life long" – have beliefs entailing its negation and will thus remain in unresolved conflict with himself: if he jettisons the premises from which Socrates deduced the negation of p in any given elenchus, there will "always" be other beliefs within him from which the same result may be obtained.

If this is what Socrates assumes, why does he not argue for it? Because it is a meta-elenctic statement.[65] To support it Socrates would have to engage in meta-elenctic inquiry. And this, as I indicated at the start of this chapter, Socrates never does in Plato's earlier dialogues. In every one of them prior to the *Meno* Socrates maintains epistemological innocence, methodological naivety. He

---

[65]   That is why I ignored it in my account of standard elenchus at the start of section II above. It *should* be ignored in the analysis of the logical structure of any given elenctic argument: [A] is not a premise in any elenctic argument, nor does Socrates suggest that it is. The remarks from which I have teased it out are *obiter dicta*. The interlocutor would be perfectly justified if he ignored them as pure Socratic bluster: he has been given no reason why *he* should think them true. That is why [A] has been brought in only to explain *why Socrates himself believes* that to prove the inconsistency of the thesis with the agreed-upon premises is *ipso facto* to prove that, if the thesis is false, no one can affirm it without generating contradiction within his own system of belief, and in this way to "prove" the thesis false (T19 above).

assumes he has the right method to search for moral truth, but never attempts to justify the assumption. *A fortiori* he never attempts to justify the assumption on which the constructive efficacy of the method is predicated. This is not to say that the assumption is arbitrary. He does have this much reason for [A]: every time he tangles with people who defend a thesis he considers false and he looks for premises among their own beliefs from which he can derive its negation, the needed premises are in place – they are always where they ought to be if [A] is true. So he has this purely inductive evidence for a part of [A] – for all of it except the claim in [A] that the beliefs from which he deduces the negation of his interlocutors' theses are *true*.[66] For this he would have to fall back on nothing better than the pragmatic value of those beliefs: they articulate intuitions which prove practically viable in his own experience; they tell him who is happy and who isn't; he does what they tell him and he *is* happy.[67]

Here we come within sight of the solution of "the problem of the elenchus." To reach it we should note that from assumption [A] Socrates could infer securely that any set of moral beliefs which was internally consistent would contain exclusively true beliefs: for if it contained even a single false belief, then, given [A], it would have to contain beliefs entailing the negation of that false belief. Let us then look at part [a] of T24. What can Socrates mean by telling Callicles that what he had heard from Socrates in his argument against Polus had been spoken by "philosophy," setting himself up, so very arrogantly it seems, as mouthpiece of the very process by which moral truth is reached? The things Callicles is said to have heard from "philosophy" are the theses Socrates has defended against Polus and stands ready to defend against everyone else. The salient feature of those assertions of his which he exalts by saying that they were spoken by "philosophy" is their mutual consistency: his love, philosophy, he says "always says the same thing"; by implication, so does

---

[66] At this point I am much indebted to helpful criticism from Brickhouse and Smith (1984: 187–92). They convinced me that the contrary view I had expressed in the earlier version of this paper was wrong, and I withdrew it in my next publication (1985: 18–19 = ch. 2, pp. 56–7).

[67] Cf. *Socrates*, "Epilogue: Felix Socrates."

Socrates too.[68] He asserts this flatly a little later (490E 10–11), assuring Callicles that he, unlike Callicles, always says the same things about the same things.

In the immediate sequel to T24[b], he proceeds to elevate consistency to a supreme desideratum in his own search for truth:

T24[c] *G.* 482B–C: "As for me, I would rather that my lyre were out of tune and discordant or a choir I was directing, and that a whole multitude should dissent from me and contradict me, than that I, a single man, should be out of tune with myself and contradict myself."

For years he has been striving for just this, constantly exposing the consistency of his beliefs to elenctic challenge, ready to root out any belief, however attractive in itself, which if allowed to stand would disturb the coherence of the system as a whole. So this is where he now finds himself after all those years of searching: of all the sets of moral beliefs competing for acceptance in elenctic argument, only one has shown up in his own experience that meets this desideratum – his own. All others, when tested for consistency, have failed. So he has evidence – as before, inductive evidence,[69] – for a further assumption:

---

[68] No one should be misled by his retrospective remark (527D), "we never think the same about the same things." As Dodds, 1959, remarks *ad loc.*, "this reproach applies of course to Callicles only ..., but Socrates politely includes himself." For similarly ironical substitution of "we" for "you" see *Eu.* 15C8–9, "Either we were wrong when we agreed before or, if we were right then, we are wrong now" (as the context shows "we" in its last occurrence refers exclusively to Euthyphro); *Ch.* 175B6–7, "We have admitted that there is knowledge of knowledge although the argument said 'No'" (it was only Critias who had argued for "knowledge of knowledge": Socrates had argued "No"); *La.* 194C, "Come, Nicias, rescue, if you can, your friends storm-tossed in the argument" (only Laches had been "storm-tossed"; Socrates, sailing very smoothly, had done the rebutting). The irony at *G.* 527D should be transparent: Callicles had been convicted of numerous inconsistencies, Socrates of not even one. Kraut, 1983: 69, missing its irony, takes this text to be "as clear a confession of inconsistency as we could want." (Alternatively, Socrates may use "we" when "I" is unambiguously what he means, as at *Eu.* 6B: "we who ourselves agree that we know nothing of such things [strife among the gods]." Euthyphro had agreed to nothing of the kind; he knows altogether too much about them: 5E–6A).

[69] The consistency of the set is being inferred from its track-record in Socrates' own experience: in all of the elenctic arguments in which he has engaged he has never been faulted for inconsistency. This is a very chancy inference, for the results of elenctic argument are powerfully affected by the argumentative skill of the contestants; since that of Socrates vastly exceeds that of his interlocutors, he is more effective in finding beliefs of theirs which entail the negation of their thesis than are they when trying to do the same to him. So his undefeated record need not show that his belief-set is consistent; it may only show that its inconsistencies have defied the power of his adversaries to ferret them out. Socrates could hardly have been unaware of this unavoidable hazard in his method. This must contribute to the sense of its fallibility which, I believe, is the right clue to his profession of ignorance.

[B]   The set of elenctically tested moral beliefs held by Socrates at any given time is consistent.

Socrates would not wish to say, and never does say, that he *knows* that all of his moral beliefs are mutually consistent.[70] All he need say is that he believes that this is so and that this, like all of his other beliefs, is subject to elenctic challenge by all comers, inviting its refutation by anyone who can show that one or more of the beliefs within the set entail the negation of one or more others in it. So long as consistency of the set stands proof against all challenges, Socrates would be perfectly justified in holding assumption [B] and hence in supposing, in consequence of assumption [A], that his belief-set consists exclusively of true beliefs.

This last move yields the missing piece required for the solution of "the problem of the elenchus." The puzzle arises over Socrates' claim at (4) in the above analysis of standard elenchus (p. 11): when he has shown that *not-p* follows from *q* and *r*, for whose truth he has not argued, why should he want to claim that his argument has "proved" *not-p* true? What makes him think it has? The answer is in assumptions [A] and [B] whose conjunction, as I have just pointed out, entails that Socrates' belief-set consists entirely of true beliefs, from which it follows that *q* and *r* are true: to show that *not-p* follows from premises which are true, *is* to prove *not-p* true.[71]

Imagine now Plato writing Socratic dialogues. Under the influence of a certain Cratylus he had once become convinced that there can be no knowledge of the sensible world because it is all in flux,[72] and this had left him wondering how there could be any knowledge of anything at all. The Socrates he brings to life in dialogue after dialogue disclaims that he has knowledge but nonetheless searches indefatigably for moral truth, and in the *Gorgias* he sees it findable in the most unlikely of all places – in the minds of those

---

[70] That Socrates should accept [B] and base on it his confidence that he can prove his theses true and nonetheless deny that he knows that [B] is true may seem astonishing. It is no more so than his maintaining that he can prove his theses true but does not know that they are true: see additional note 1.3 below, "On *Gorgias* 508E–509A."

[71] Which explains why Socrates should want to say to Callicles: "If you agree with the things my soul believes, these things will be the very truth" (*G.* 486E) and "your agreement will reach the goal of truth" (*G.* 487E). Cf. chapter 2, comment on the text cited there as T12.

[72] Aristotle, *Metaph.* 987a32ff., with comment *ad loc.* by Ross, 1924.

misguided, confused, wrong-headed people whose souls he seeks to improve. The question, "How could this be true?", which never disturbed Socrates, could hardly help disturbing Plato when he writes the *Gorgias*. For here he puts into Socrates' mouth that flock of *obiter dicta* which reveal the assumptions on which he predicates his confidence that the elenctic method establishes truth and falsehood.

Then, one day, Plato becomes convinced of something his teacher would have thought fantastic – that every person's soul had existed long before birth, had gone through many previous births into different incarnations and had acquired, in some mysterious way, prenatal knowledge *about everything*,[73] and this knowledge was now in every soul and fragments of it were recoverable through "recollection." Would not this have struck Plato as answering the question he never makes Socrates ask: how could it have happened that each and every one of Socrates' interlocutors did have those true beliefs he needs to refute all of their false ones? That wildest of Plato's metaphysical flights, that ultra-speculative theory that all learning is "recollection," is understandable as, among other things, an answer to a problem in Socratic elenchus.

APPENDIX: THE DEMISE OF THE ELENCHUS IN THE *EUTHYDEMUS*, *LYSIS*, AND *HIPPIAS MAJOR*

It had long passed unnoticed in the scholarly literature[1] that these three dialogues, each of which had been frequently thought (on the

---

[73] "The soul, being immortal and having had many births, and having seen everything both in this world and in Hades, *there is nothing it has not come to know*" (*Meno* 81c5–7). In *Socrates* (ch. 2, n. 32) I emphasized that there is no evidence of acceptance of this extraordinary doctrine in the Platonic corpus prior to the *Meno*, hence none of its acceptance in the *Gorgias*: the eschatological myth with which this dialogue concludes is "a purely moral fable, an embroidery on the popular belief ... in a retributive post-mortem trial ... – a belief with rich moral content and no epistemic import" (*loc. cit.*).

[1] There had been no mention of it prior to the publication of the original version of the present Appendix (1983).

strength of miscellaneous criteria) to fall late within the earlier dialogues,[2] have a common feature which distinguishes them from all of
the other dialogues in this group: abandonment of adversary argument as Socrates' method of philosophical investigation. The theses
which are seriously debated in these dialogues are uncontested by
the interlocutor; Socrates himself is both their author and critic.

EUTHYDEMUS

Prevented by the eristic clowning of the two sophists from using
elenctic refutation against them, Socrates does the serious business of
the dialogue in a protreptic discourse to young Cleinias. Here the
only theses investigated by Socrates are introduced, argued for, examined, and amended by himself in the didactic style of the middle
dialogues, where the interlocutor is a yes-man, who may ask questions and occasionally raise objections, but never puts up sustained
resistance to a Socratic thesis. Cleinias, a teenager, is docility itself.
When he does contribute something of his own (to everyone's surprise), it is to anticipate the very thing that is needed to round out
Socrates' thought (290B–D). A further way in which Socrates now
breaks with the modalities of elenctic argument is to ground his
doctrine in a proposition – the universal desire for happiness – which
he presents as uncontestable in principle: to question it, he says,
would be "ridiculous" and "senseless" (278E4–5). Such a move is
never made in a preceding dialogue: there everything is contestable.

LYSIS

Here again there is no elenchus against anybody – not even *pro forma*
and for comic effect, as in the *Hippias Major*. In the initial encounter

---

[2] On the *Eud.*, writes Guthrie, 1975: 266, "the prevailing opinion [reviewed in Keulen 1971]
is that the *Euthydemus*, like the *Meno*, was written after the early Socratic dialogues and the
Protagoras, but before the great central group." On the *Ly.* see especially the useful review of
work on this dialogue in Schoplick, 1969, supporting the conclusion that the *Ly.* is closely
related to the *Eud.* and probably comes before the *M.* but after the *G.* The fullest case for the
HMa. as a transitional dialogue is made in Woodruff, 1982; 175–9; it would have been
strengthened considerably if he had noticed that 303B–C contain a clear reference to a
theorem about irrationals, the earliest evidence in the corpus of Plato's knowledge of advanced developments in contemporary mathematics which he will be displaying in great
abundance in the *M.*

with Hippothales what the love-crazed youth gets is not a refutation (he has proposed no thesis) but a dressing down. When the investigation gets under way Socrates proposes all the theses which are discussed and refutes all the theses which are refuted. There is no contest. When Socrates proposes a thesis the amiable teenagers (whose strong point is good manners and good looks, not brains) go along; when he turns against it they are surprised (215C, 218D), but immediately fall in with Socrates' new move and tag along.[3]

HIPPIAS MAJOR

After regaling Hippias with fulsome compliments whose irony is lost on the sophist, the "What is the *F*?" question is sprung. Socrates makes sport with Hippias' ludicrously inept answers (they are the goofiest definitions in the corpus) while trying to get him to grasp what is called for in a definition[4] and then cashiers him as sponsor of discussable answers to the "What is the *F*?" question. Definitions meant to be taken seriously – the "fitting" (293Dff.), the "useful" (295Cff.), "that which pleases through eyesight or hearing" (297Eff.) – are all put forward by Socrates, encountering no resistance from Hippias, and are refuted by Socrates' *alter ego*, that vulgar, hybristic "relative" of his, who terrorizes him and even threatens to thrash him for his stupidity. It is as if Plato were saying: my Socrates has now come to see that elenctic refutation of others is not worth much; it is his own self-criticism that he must meet to make progress towards the truth.

Thus in these three works, all of which must precede the *Meno*, for none of them anticipates its metaphysical, epistemological, and methodological novelties, Socrates ditches the elenchus. It is a reasonable conjecture that it is Plato himself who has now lost faith in the elenchus and extricates his Socrates from it, allowing him to move out of it quietly, without comment, without saying that he is doing so, and *a fortiori* without explaining why.

As to the relative order of the three dialogues, and the relation of

[3] Cf. Shorey, 1933: 490, on *Ly.* 218B–C: "Observe the readiness with which interlocutors accept what Socrates suggests and then are dashed by his discovery of new objections."
[4] Cf. n. 22 in ch. 1 above.

all three to the *Meno*,[5] there is this much to be said for the one in
which I have taken them up in this Appendix: the attitude of the
Hippias Major to the "What is the *F*?" question is furthest removed
from the one maintained towards it in the elenctic dialogues. In
none of these had Socrates regarded the aporetic conclusion as anything worse than a temporary setback in his search for the definition:
he had voiced disappointment that the search had failed on the
present occasion, not despair that it could ever succeed. This remains as true of the *Euthydemus* as of any of its predecessors. At
292E Socrates declares that he has come "less than halfway to learning what is that knowledge which will make us happy." But he does
not say that he is giving up the search. He is ready to go on and
would do so on the spot, if only the sophists would sober up and join
in. Though his appeal for "instruction" from them is heavily ironical, it conveys no indication that success depends on them.

Moreover in none of those dialogues, including the *Euthydemus*, is
the failure of any given search regarded as portending a moral
collapse: from his failure to discover the answer to "What is piety?"
in the *Euthyphro*, to "What is courage?" in the *Laches*, to "What
is *sophrosyne*?" in the *Charmides*, to "What is the knowledge that
makes us happy?" in the *Euthydemus*, Socrates doesn't conclude that
his own ability to make personal judgments about the piety or courage or *sophrosyne* or moral knowledge achieved or missed in any
given action, his own or another's, has been discredited. This is
precisely what he infers in the *Hippias Major*: his failure to find the
answer to "What is the *kalon*?" after the long search for it in this
dialogue prompts him to conclude (304D8–E2) that he is no longer
in a position to judge whether or not any action is *kalon*. Similarly in
the *Lysis* the failure to answer "What is the *philon*?" leads him to say
in the dialogue's concluding sentence that he is no longer able to say
that the youths are each others' friends and he theirs. In the *Hippias*

---

[5] That this is later than all three is a reasonable inference from (a) the announcement in the
Meno, for the first time in Plato's corpus, of the "recollecting," transmigrating soul, a
cardinal doctrine of his middle period, and (b) the copious display in the *Meno* of advanced
mathematical knowledge, in which Socrates had never shown either interest or proficiency
in the elenctic dialogues, but which he will be requiring of all philosophers in book VII of the
Republic: there is a flash of this in the *HMa*. (cf. n. 2 above *sub fin*.), the first in the corpus,
giving us reason for regarding the *HMa*. as the last before the *Meno*.

Major the practical implications of that conclusion are more sweeping and dramatically emphatic. They are so devastating as to leave him with the question, "If this is to be your condition, is life now better for you than death?" (304E2–3).[6]

POSTSCRIPT TO "THE SOCRATIC ELENCHUS"

In the *Gorgias*, no less than in dialogues which precede it,[1] Socrates propounds with great assurance radically new moral doctrine, yet professes not to know if that doctrine is true.[2] When Dodds[3] hailed the Socrates of the *Gorgias* as the prophet of a new life, he should not have ignored the fact that the same could be said of the Socrates of the *Crito*: in his root-and-branch rejection of the *lex talionis*[4] Socrates moves there against traditional morality as defiantly as in anything he says in the *Gorgias*.[5] Neither should Dodds have suggested that the "positiveness" of the *Gorgias* supersedes the disavowal of knowledge: the profession of ignorance is reaffirmed as firmly as before.[6] Even so, there are residual differences.

(1) Only in the *Gorgias* does Socrates say that his theses have been

---

[6] This text, whose importance has never been recognized in the scholarly literature, will be further discussed in ch. 3 below.
[1] That the *G.* is preceded by {*Ap., Ch., Cr., Eu., HMi., Ion, La., Pr.*}, as in Brandwood, 1976: xvii; Dodds, 1959: 18ff.; Irwin, 1979: 5–8, is now widely recognized. (With the early dialogues I have just listed I would also group *R.* 1. See *Socrates*, additional note 2.1.) The attempt by Kahn, 1981: *passim*, to predate the *G.* to a position immediately following the *Ap.* and the *Cr.* has not to my knowledge gained a single adherent in the critical literature.
[2] See additional note 1.3.
[3] 1959: 16 *et passim*.
[4] *Cr.* 49C10–D9; and cf. *Socrates*, ch. 7, "Socrates' rejection of retaliation."
[5] He says that those who cannot agree with him on this against "the multitude" can have no common deliberation with him about anything (*Cr.* 49D2–5).
[6] "I do not speak as one who has knowledge" (506A3–4); "but, as for me, my position is always the same: I do not know how these things are" (509A). Dodds' dismissive comment (*ad loc.*) on the latter text ("It is as if Plato had belatedly remembered to make his hero speak in character") begs the question (how are we supposed to know that the disclaimer represents only a "belated" afterthought?) and, in any case, disregards the equally strong disclaimer at 506A which passes unglossed in Dodds' commentary.

"proved" true[7] or, equivalently, by a powerful metaphor, "have been clamped down and bound by arguments of iron and adamant" (508E–509A). In previous dialogues he prefers weaker rhetoric, describing the elenctic refutation of *p* by saying that *not-p* "has become evident to us (ἐφάνη ἡμῖν),"[8] or that the interlocutor now "sees"[9] or "knows"[10] that *not-p*. How substantial is the difference? Since we are given no analysis of what we are to understand by proof, we cannot be sure. Even so, the difference in tone is unmistakable. And when both kinds of language are used in close juxtaposition it does look as though "*not-p* has been proved true" is meant to be stronger in some unspecified way than is "*not-p* has been made evident":

T1[11] *G.* 508E–509A: "These things having become evident (φανέντα) in the foregoing arguments, I would say, crude though it may seem to say it, that they *have been clamped down and bound by arguments of iron and adamant.*"

The second of these two claims – the one I have italicized – strikes Socrates as so much stronger than the first that he feels he is risking a breach of good manners in voicing it so flamboyantly.[12]

(2) Only in the *Gorgias* do we encounter those texts from which we can tell that Socrates now is knowingly committed to that extraordinary idea which, transposed into more abstract language, has been formalized as assumption [A] in chapter 1 above. Not one of those texts is paralleled in any earlier dialogue. Nowhere but in the *Gorgias* does Socrates give any clear sign of holding that the truth he presses on his adversaries is already *in* them, despite their stubborn resistance to it – that they already "believe" it and can be compelled by elenctic parley to "witness" for it;[13] that unless they recognize

---

[7] 479E, cited in T19 in chapter 1 above. In the *Pr.* it is Socrates' opponent who so refers to the conclusion of the Socratic argument (ἀπεδείχθη, 359D) and though Socrates does not demur, neither does he affirm it categorically.

[8] *Pr.* 353B3–4; *Eu.* 15C1–2; *R.* I, 335E5. ἐφάνη without the personal pronoun in the dative (which is understood in context): *Eu.* 9C7–8; *R.* I, 336A9; καταφανὲς γενέσθαι, *R.* I, 347D4; γίγνεσθαι καταφανές, *Ch.* 166D5–6.

[9] ὁρᾷς, *Eu.* 11A3.

[10] ἴστε, *Pr.* 357E1.

[11] Quoted in additional note 1.3. [GV did not live to bring the translation he gave in additional note 1.3 into line with the version quoted above, which reflects his most recent thinking on the text. – Ed.]

[12] As Dodds (1959, *ad loc.*) remarks, it is not, as some have thought, the boldness of the metaphor, but "the arrogance of the expression" that calls for apology.

[13] Texts T23 and T20, T21 in ch. 1 above.

its truth they doom themselves to a life of unacknowledged self-contradiction.[14]

What do these differences come to? Is Plato telling us that Socrates has now become more confident of the truth of his moral theses and of the efficacy of his elenctic method in reaching that truth? Decidedly not. In dialogues, like the *Euthyphro* and the *Crito* whose dramatic date comes well after that of the *Gorgias*,[15] Socrates is as positive as before about major doctrines – that piety is god-loved because it is piety, not vice versa (*Eu.* 11A); that returning wrong for wrong and evil for evil is unconditionally unjust (*Cr.* 49C–D). And since those doctrines are presented as conclusions reached by the elenctic method, the efficacy of that method is implicitly recommended as confidently as in the *Gorgias*. Nor could Plato be telling us that at the time of Socrates' life depicted in the *Gorgias* his old teacher had suddenly become more self-conscious about the presuppositions of his method than he had been before. Such a hypothesis, requiring enhancement of self-consciousness at a certain point of Socrates' life, and then its loss thereafter, would make poor sense. So we are driven to the alternative hypothesis, which makes perfect sense, that it is *Plato*, not Socrates, who reached that new insight into his teacher's method when he wrote the *Gorgias*, and that he put it into his text in just that dialogue, because what became clear to him then had not done so before.

Throughout the preceding dialogues Plato depicts Socrates arguing for his views much as other philosophers have done before or since when trying to bring others around to their own view of a disputed matter. So far as he can, he picks premises so eminently reasonable in themselves and so well-entrenched in his interlocutors' beliefs, that when he faces them with the fact that these premises entail the negation of their thesis he feels no serious risk that they will renege on the premises to save the thesis – as in fact they never do. What I said in section III of chapter 1 above they *could* always do, if they so chose, not once does any of them do. Fume or squirm as

---

[14] Quoted in T24[b] in ch. 1.

[15] Which Plato makes no effort to fix with any definiteness: see the "Note on the dramatic date" of the *Gorgias* in Dodds, 1959: 17–18. But it is in any case distinctly earlier than that of *Apology* and the *Crito*, whose time-frame puts them within the last days of Socrates' life.

they may at the outcome of the argument, Socrates expects them to stick by the agreed-upon premises, and his expectation is never disappointed.

This being the case, the "problem of the elenchus" never bothers Socrates in those earlier dialogues. Why should it? He has a method that works well enough for his own purposes. It organizes his moral intuitions into a set which is reassuringly consistent and, moreover, proves practically viable in his own experience. Drawing the premises of his elenctic arguments from this set, he makes sufficient contact with beliefs firmly lodged in the mind of dissenting interlocutors to drive them into impasse in argument after argument; and since, when he has got them cornered, they do not welsh on premises to which they have agreed, he infers that the falsehood of their thesis has now been made "evident" to them by his argument. So why should he be puzzled?

If he were an epistemologist, he might well have asked, "What reason is there to believe that those who disagree with me must have those entrenched beliefs which I can use to make them 'see' the falsehood their misguided theses?" But since he is no epistemologist, he doesn't raise that question. And if he doesn't, why should he be worried? It must be Plato, then, who comes to feel the force of that question when he writes the *Gorgias*. It now dawns on him that the elenchus had been predicated on frightfully strong assumptions, notably [A]: if, as Socrates had believed, his theses are universally certifiable by the elenctic method,[16] they should be provable *to anyone*, hence *everyone* must have the true beliefs entailing the negation of each of his false beliefs. So [A] is Plato's present to his teacher, bestowed on him in the *Gorgias*, where he is made to say those very strong things – T19, T20, T21, T22, T23, T24[a, b], and *G.* 486E–487E (cf. n. 71 above) – of which there is no sign earlier on.

To continue the scenario: when Plato sees how strong is that assumption and comes to feel it would be hopeless to try to justify it by the inductive evidence Socrates could have offered for it – extrap-

---

16 *Ch.* 166D: "Or don't you think it is a common good for practically all men that the truth in each case should be made evident?" On this point the *Charmides* is no different from the *Gorgias*: "I think we should be contentiously eager to come to know what is true and what is false about the things we discuss: for it is a common good for all that the truth should be made evident" (*G.* 505E).

olation from his personal experience – he begins to lose faith in the elenchus. The *coup de grâce* to this faith is then delivered by something new in Plato's life: his immersion in mathematical studies which, as I have argued in *Socrates*,[17] leads him out of the elenchus into a new method he learns from the mathematicians, "investigating from a hypothesis,"[18] which practices systematically what the elenchus forbids on principle: argument from an unasserted premise. So Plato proceeds to disengage Socrates from the elenchus, which he does in the *Lysis*, *Euthydemus*, and *Hippias Major*.[19] After its euthanasia in these three dialogues, the elenchus, resurrected briefly in the *Meno*, is shown to lead to an impasse, escape from which is found through a further, still more lavish, present to Socrates: the transmigration of the soul and the theory of recollection. By the time this has happened the moralist of the earlier dialogues has become the metaphysician and epistemologist of the middle ones. The metamorphosis of Plato's teacher into Plato's mouthpiece is complete.

[17] Chapter 4, "Elenchus and mathematics."
[18] ἐξ ὑποθέσεως σκοπεῖσθαι, *M.* 86ε3.
[19] As I have argued in the Appendix above and, more fully, in "Elenchus and mathematics" (cf. n. 17 above).

2

SOCRATES' DISAVOWAL OF
KNOWLEDGE

In Plato's earliest dialogues,[1] when Socrates says he has no knowledge, does he or does he not mean what he says? The standard view has been that he does not. What can be said for this interpretation is well said in Gulley, 1968: Socrates' profession of ignorance is "an expedient to encourage his interlocutor to seek out the truth, to make him think that he is joining with Socrates in a voyage of discovery" (p. 69). More recently the opposite interpretation has found a clear-headed advocate. Terence Irwin in his *Plato's Moral Theory*[2] holds that when Socrates disclaims knowledge he should be taken at his word: he has renounced knowledge and is content to claim no more than true belief (Irwin, 1977: 39–40).

I shall argue that when each of these views is confronted with the textual evidence each is proved false: there are texts which falsify the first, and others which falsify the second. How could this be? These views are proper contradictories: if either is false, must not the other be true? Not necessarily. If Socrates is making appropriately variable use of his words for "knowing"[3] both views could be false. I shall argue that this is in fact the case, proposing a hypothesis which

---

[1] See additional note 1.1.

[2] My debt to this book is very great. Only those who are strangers to the ethos of scholarly controversy will see anything but high esteem in my critique of it here and in a parallel essay, "Happiness and virtue in Socrates' moral theory," in *Socrates*, chapter 8.

[3] The verbs, ἐπίσταμαι, οἶδα, γιγνώσκω, ἐπαΐω, and their cognate nouns, if any; the adjective σοφός, and the noun σοφία, which is used as interchangeable with ἐπιστήμη (as e.g. at *Ap.* 23A7: here ἐπιστήμη could have been substituted for σοφία *salva veritate*, as it in fact is at 19C6).

explains why Socrates should wish to do just this.[4] I shall review the
relevant evidence (section I), develop the hypothesis (section II), and
exhibit its explanatory power (section III).

I

The first interpretation is virtually ubiquitous. It has even captured
the dictionaries. *Webster's* gives this entry under "irony":

T1   A pretence of ignorance and of willingness to learn from another assumed
in order to make the other's false conception conspicuous by adroit reasoning –
called also "Socratic irony."

The *O.E.D.* gives the same explanation for the "etymological sense"
of "irony":

T2   Dissimulation, pretence; especially [of] ignorance feigned by Socrates as a
means of confuting an adversary (Socratic irony).

"Pretence" is the key word here. Socrates is dissembling, though for
excellent reasons. To the pedagogical ones adduced by Gulley might
be added Socrates' interest in maneuvering his interlocutors into the
answerer's role, so he may keep the questioner's for himself. Aristotle
attests this use of the disclaimer:

T3 *Soph. El.* 183b7–8:   ... Socrates asked questions but gave no replies: for he
confessed (ὡμολόγει) he had no knowledge.

But Aristotle is not implying that the disclaimer was a pretence.[5] His
wording strongly suggests the opposite.[6] The same suggestion is conveyed by a writer of Socratic dialogues contemporary with Plato's:

---

[4] This proposal breaks with previous interpretations (with all of those known to me), including an earlier one of mine (in Vlastos, 1956: xxx–xxxi), where I conflated two distinct
claims: that Socrates renounces certainty (which is true) *and* knowledge (which is false).
Gulley fell into the same trap. He assumed that his (perfectly valid) critique of the second
claim also disposes of the first.

[5] Quite the contrary: as Gulley notes (p. 62), Aristotle cites Socrates as one who argues
without having knowledge of the subject under discussion – not ὡς εἰδώς, but "peirastically"
(*Soph. El.*183a39ff.). Cf. my discussion of this point in ch. 1, p. 16 above.

[6] ὡμολόγει (in past imperfect: "he used to confess"). For "pretended" or "feigned' Aristotle
would have written προσεποιεῖτο: he uses this verb repeatedly in his discussion of the εἴρων
in *N.E.* 1127b10ff. (and προσποίησις in 1108a21) and in *Magna Mor.* 1193a28ff. (note also
the use of ὁμολογεῖν in contrast to προσποιεῖσθαι in the description of the ἀληθευτικός, *N.E.*
1127a25, τὰ ὑπάρχοντα ὁμολογῶν). For Aristotle Socrates is indeed an εἴρων, but *not* for
disavowing knowledge: nowhere does he bring the profession of ignorance under the "disclaimer of prestigious qualities" which he ascribes to Socrates *qua* εἴρων.

T4 Aeschines Socraticus, *Alcibiades* (fragment 10C, Dittmar): "I had no knowledge I could teach the man to improve him, but I thought that by associating with him I could improve him through my love."

In Plato the only character who says that Socrates is feigning ignorance is Thrasymachus:

T5 *R.* I, 337A3–7: "When he heard this he gave a great sardonic horse-laugh and said: 'Heracles! this is Socrates' customary feigning (εἰρωνεία).' I had predicted this – I had told the people here that you would not want to give answers and would dissemble (εἰρωνεύσοιο) and would do anything but answer if you are questioned."[7]

But Socrates does not agree, nor does anyone friendly to him. If we were to believe Thrasymachus, we would have to do so without support from any of our earliest sources.

And we would have much explaining to do. How could Socrates be dissembling – saying what he does not believe – when his own first rule in elenctic dialogue is "say what you believe"?[8] And how would we account for the pretence in circumstances in which it cannot be meant to bring the interlocutor into the answerer's role? So, notably, at the conclusion of the debate with Callicles. Why should Socrates say *then*, "I do not assert the things I say as one who knows" (*G.* 506A3–4), and again three pages later, after declaring that his theses have now been "bound and clamped down by arguments of iron and adamant" (508E–509A), why should he then add,

T6 *G.* 509A4–5: "But as for me my position (λόγος) is always the same.[9] I do not know how these things are."[10]

---

[7] Here εἰρωνεία clearly means "dissembling." It is given this sense in the translations by Cornford, Lindsay, and Robin, but is mistranslated as "irony" in the ones by Bloom, Grube, Shorey, possibly because the conceptual difference between *irony* and *dissembling* is not observed: the intention to deceive, built into the meaning of the latter, must be absent from the former ("What fine weather!," said while it is raining cats and dogs, is not meant to fool anybody). εἰρωνεία straddles this difference, hence Plato may use it for either dissembling (as here and sometimes elsewhere: *Sph.* 268B–C, *Lg.* 908E) or irony (as quite clearly in *Smp.* 218D6 and *G.* 489E1–3, less clearly in *Ap.* 38A, *Smp.* 216E4).

[8] *Cr.* 49C–D; *Pr.* 331C; *R.* I 337C, 346A, 350A; *G.* 495A, 500B. And see the discussion of this rule in ch. 1 above.

[9] The λόγος at 509A4 is not the theses he has defended against Callicles (to these he refers by ταῦτα at A5, as previously at 508E6 and subsequently at 509B1), but his disavowal of knowledge (cf. οὐδὲ εἰδὼς λέγω at 506A3 with λόγος ὅτι οὐκ οἶδα here). Nor is λόγος being used here to mean "argument" (so translated by Irwin, 1979); Socrates disavows knowledge here and at 506A3–4, but does not argue for the disavowal.

[10] This disavowal, so unqualified on the face of it, Gulley, 1968: 69, dismisses by a complicated exegetical maneuver, borrowed from Dodds, 1959: 341. For my critique of it see my retort to Dodds in Postscript to 'The Socratic elenchus,'" p. 33 above.

If the disavowal is false, why dish out the falsehood at this late moment in the debate?

But we have not yet reached the strongest evidence that the disavowal is sincere. It comes in the *Apology*. Chaerephon had asked at Delphi, "Is there anyone wiser than Socrates?" And the oracle had said, "No."

That answer, Socrates tells the jury, plunged him into prolonged perplexity:

T7 *Ap.* 21B2–5:   "When I heard this I kept thinking: 'What on earth does the god mean? What is he hinting at? For I am aware of not being wise in anything, great or small. What then could he mean by saying that I am wise?' "

Could Socrates have said *to himself*, "I am aware of not being wise in anything," if he thought it untrue? The same question arises again a few lines later as Socrates narrates the outcome of his first encounter with a victim of conceit of knowledge:

T8 *Ap.* 21D2–6:   "As I was going away from this man I reasoned to myself that I am indeed wiser than he. It is unlikely that either of us knows anything noble or good. But he, having no knowledge, thinks he knows something, while I, having none, don't think I have any."

What would we make of that narrated soliloquy on the hypothesis that Socratic ignorance is feigned? Is the narrative meant to be fact or fiction? If fiction, Socrates is lying to the judges, to whom he had promised, just a moment earlier (20D): "Now I shall tell you the whole truth." If fact – if the story is meant to be true – then Socrates would have had to believe that he had performed an unperformable speech-act, namely, that he had knowingly dissembled to himself.

Let us then consider the alternative hypothesis – that "Socrates claims no knowledge for himself ... He allows both his interlocutors and himself true beliefs without knowledge."[11] If so, how is it that

---

[11] Irwin, 1977: 40–1. Though Irwin's is the only argued-out defense of this view in the scholarly literature, I have the impression that it is widely shared. It is conceded in Burnyeat, 1977: 384ff.; the concession, incidental to his discussion of the "Socratic fallacy," is not argued for on its own account. It is as marginal (and more hesitant) in Santas, 1979: 119ff. and 311, n. 26. To Irwin's argument I cannot do detailed justice. Constraints of space allow me no more than a remark and a more general reflection.

(1) While his thesis is a perfectly reasonable conclusion from the texts he cites, that textual base is incomplete: missing from it are a series of texts (also unnoticed by Burnyeat and Santas) where Socrates, though stopping short of asserting explicitly that he has moral knowledge, nevertheless implies it unambiguously (T12–T17 below). (I shall expound (1) at length, devoting to it the rest of the present section.)

what he keeps searching for throughout his life is not true belief, but knowledge?

T9 *G*. 505E4–5: "I think we should be contentiously eager *to know* what is true and what is false about the things we discuss..."

T10 *G*. 472C6–D1: "For the things we are debating are ... things which *to know* is noblest, not *to know* most base. For their sum and substance is this: *to know* or not *to know* who is happy and who is not."

If after decades of searching Socrates remained convinced that he still knew *nothing*,[12] would not further searching have become a charade – or rather worse? For he holds that virtue "is" knowledge: if he has no knowledge, his life is a disaster, he has missed out on virtue and, therewith, on happiness. How is it then that he is serenely confident he has achieved both?[13]

In any case, there is a familiar text where Socrates says flatly that he knows a moral truth:

T11 *Ap*. 29B6–7: "... but that to do injustice and disobey my superior, god or man, this I *know* to be evil and base."

This single text, if given its full weight, would suffice to show that Socrates claims knowledge of a moral truth. Irwin denies it any

(2) I surmise that Irwin and those who agree with him are conflating the claim to knowledge with the claim to certainty, as Gulley and I did earlier on (cf. n. 4 above). Once one comes to realize that Socrates can avow knowledge on the basis of nothing better than fallibly justifiable true belief (as I shall be arguing he does: section II below), one is less likely to dismiss or bypass those texts in which Socrates says or implies that he has knowledge on the strength of nothing better.

12 "Absolutely nothing" is the clear import of T7 and T8, whose force has been blunted past all recognition in scholarly comment on it, as e.g. Zeller, 1885: 124 (I have added the reference marks): "[a] Socrates really knew nothing, or, to express it otherwise, [b] he had no developed theory, and no positive dogmatic principles." Who would have thought that a serious philosopher might have said [a] and *meant* [b]? Similar emasculations of Socrates' avowal of ignorance abound in the scholarly literature; for a fair sample see the exposition of what W. K. C. Guthrie terms "the ignorance of Socrates" in Guthrie, 1969: 442ff.

13 His avowals of epistemic inadequacy, frequent in the dialogues, are never paralleled by admission of moral failure; the asymmetry is striking. He will face the last judgment confident that "he has never wronged man or god in word or deed" (*G*. 522D); he is convinced that "he does no wrong to anyone" (*Ap*. 37B2–3). That he does not say he *knows* this (as Irwin observes, 1977: 294) is no objection: being convinced of *p* is consistent with knowing *p*. As for happiness, no scene recorded in the secular literature of the West portrays more compellingly serenity and even cheerfulness *in extremis* than does the death scene in the *Phaedo* (117B3, C4), which is admissible as evidence of Socrates' personal qualities: here, and also in Alcibiades' speech in the *Smp*., the personal character of Socrates survives his transformation into a mouthpiece of Platonic philosophy.

weight on the ground that it is so exceptional,[14] which, of course, it is,[15] but not as much so as he and others have thought it.

Consider what Socrates says to Callicles when their debate is about to start:

T12 *G.* 486E5–6: "I *know* well that if you will agree with me on those things which my soul believes, those things will be the very truth."[16]

To grasp the import of this text for the hypothesis that Socrates is claiming to have knowledge of moral truth we must take account of what he aims to achieve in elenctic argument and how he goes about achieving it within the framework of a standard elenchus.[17] His aim, he says, is to compel his interlocutors to "witness against themselves,"[18] i.e. to induce them to see that the falsehood of their theses is entailed by propositions presently embedded within their own system of belief – propositions they themselves consider true. To achieve this aim he figures out what premises they accept which will enable him to contrive the contradiction[19] and secure their acceptance by *ad hoc* agreement. Let p be an interlocutor's thesis which Socrates considers false, and let q and r be the premises on which agreement is reached. Does Socrates, for his part, believe that q

---

[14] 1977: 58. He gives no other reason for dismissing it.

[15] This is indeed the only place in Plato's earliest dialogues where Socrates avows flatly, without resort to indirection of any sort, that he *knows* a moral truth. Why this should have happened so rarely is an important question to which my hypothesis supplies an answer (in section III below).

[16] Inexplicably (but perhaps not unpredictably: cf. n. 11 (2) above) there is no confrontation of this text in Irwin, 1977, nor yet of the ones I shall be citing after it in the present section (T13–T17): none of them are listed in the book's (commendably full) *Index locorum*; their relevance to Irwin's thesis is ignored.

[17] For my analysis of "standard elenchus" (the usual form of elenctic argument in Plato's earliest dialogues) see ch. 1 above. I indicate there (n. 51) briefly some differences between Irwin's understanding of Socrates' use of elenchus and mine. Since they do not affect materially our differences on my present theme I simplify by ignoring them.

[18] For the references and comment see ch. 1, pp. 21–2, above.

[19] "The art of elenchus is to find premises believed by the answerer and yet entailing the contrary of his thesis" (Robinson, 1953:15). To "believed" add "and admitted." For if the answerer were to conceal his true opinion, Socrates would be stymied: he can only refute theses to which the interlocutor will own up (cf. n. 8 above). Hence Socrates' joy at meeting in the person of Callicles an adversary whose convictions are at the farthest extreme from his own and who can be counted on to blurt them out. Here Socrates will find "the stone by which they test gold" (486D3–4). What this touchstone will test will be Socrates' assumption that even the most misguided and depraved man will still carry in his own soul a residue of truth which can be shown to entail the negation of his perverse views. This is why Socrates can tell Callicles: "In your agreement and mine consummation of truth will be already attained" (487E6–7).

and *r* are true? In standard elenctic argument there can be no doubt of this: it follows from Socrates' conviction that the contradiction does more than expose inconsistency within the interlocutor's beliefs – that it refutes his thesis, as we can see, for instance, when Polus is told that the argument which faulted him "proved true" the Socratic thesis against his (*G.* 479E8). Socrates could not have said this unless he were convinced that *q* and *r* which are shown to entail *not-p* are themselves true. Would he be prepared to say that he *knows* they are true? Just this is what we learn from T12: if Callicles will agree on *q* and *r*, he (Socrates)[20] "knows well" that *q* and *r* will be true. How so? What makes Socrates think he knows this? And what does he mean by saying he does? These are highly relevant questions. They will be answered in due course (n. 42 below). For the present let us be content to get no more than this out of T12: Socrates is claiming to *know* that the premises to which he expects Callicles will agree are true.

Now if Socrates is assuming he knows that those premises are true, we may infer that he is also assuming he knows that the conclusions, validly deduced therefrom, are true. This inference seems safe enough. But let us not take it for granted. Is there textual evidence that Socrates makes the latter assumption? There is: for when his argument has rebutted *p*, Socrates feels entitled to assert that *not-p* has thereby "been made manifest"[21] or, equivalently, that the interlocutor now "sees" that this is the case.[22] To say this is altogether different from saying that the interlocutor has now come to believe *not-p*, which could have happened[23] for epistemically weightless

---

[20] Without implying that Callicles does so too. From "*A* knows that *p* and *B* agrees that *p*" it does not follow that "*B* knows that *p*"; and Socrates has not said that beliefs of his will be true *only* if Callicles agrees: in "if you will agree" he names a sufficient, not a necessary, condition. To serve Socrates as a "touchstone" (cf. the preceding note) Callicles needs no knowledge; his true beliefs suffice. At no point in their debate does Socrates credit Callicles with knowledge. In "you have *knowledge* and *goodwill* and *outspokenness*" (487A2–3) the mockery is as palpable in the first as in the second of the words I have italicized.

[21] ἐφάνη: φαίνομαι, in its non-dubitative sense of "come to light," "become manifest" (LSJ *sub verb.* φαίνω, passive, BI), for which its use in mathematical argument might be cited: Democritus B155 (= Plutarch, *De Commun. Notit.* 1079E): φανεῖται τὸ τοῦ κυλίνδρου πεπονθὼς ὁ κῶνος: "will manifestly have got the properties of the cylinder" (so Cherniss translates).

[22] Cf. my "Postscript to 'The Socratic elenchus,'" pp. 33ff. above.

[23] *If* it did. It might not: Callicles may be right in saying that "many" find Socrates unpersuasive (*G.* 513C5–6).

reasons – because he was cajoled or bullied or just worn down. It is to claim that he has now been given *good reason* to believe that *p* is false. And to say this is to make a knowledge-claim, if we give to "knowledge" its minimal sense of "justified true belief."[24] But is there evidence that Socrates is aware of making such a claim – that he would be prepared to say that the elenctic refutation of *p* has put the interlocutor in the position of knowing that *p* is false, and *not-p* true? There is. We see him saying as much on two occasions.

The first comes at the conclusion of his argument against "the multitude" in the *Protagoras* which establishes that wrong action (ἁμαρτάνειν) comes about not because the agent is "overcome by pleasure," as his adversaries had maintained, but because of his ignorance of the good. Socrates then proceeds to tell them that, in view of what his argument has shown,

T13 *Pr.* 357D7–E1: "You yourselves, surely, know (ἴστε που) that wrong action done without knowledge is done because of ignorance (ἀμαθίᾳ)."

In saying that *they* know this he is implying that *he* knows it, for if he did not he would have no reason for saying that they do.

Here is the second occasion: Thrasymachus' brazen claim that justice is no virtue and injustice no vice, for justice is "stupidity" and injustice "sound counsel," is attacked by a standard elenctic argument (*R.* i, 348c2–350c11), which concludes:

T14 *R.* i, 350c10–11: "Therefore, the just man has been revealed to us to be good and wise, the unjust to be ignorant and bad."

Then, a Stephanus page later, without any intervening strengthening of the argument for that conclusion, Socrates remarks:

[24] I shall be arguing that elenctically justifiable true belief makes good sense of what Socrates is claiming to have when he avows knowledge. Irwin too holds (1977: 37ff.) that the true beliefs he allows Socrates are supported by elenctic argument (cf. n. 17 above). Even so, he denies that in Socrates' view they constitute knowledge. This is the crux of our dispute. This is not whether "justified true belief" is an acceptable sense for "knowledge" in standard uses of the term (which nowadays most philosophers would deny) but rather whether Socrates (a) does avow what *he* understands by his words for "knowledge," whatever that may be, and (b) in so doing has in view nothing stronger than "justified true belief." In the case of (a) the evidence I am presenting here, never previously confronted in its entirety (especially texts T12–T17), should be conclusive. In the case of (b) I am content to argue for just that; but if a case could be made for giving Socrates' conception of knowledge the benefit of something stronger ("belief which tracks truth" as expounded by Nozick, 1981: ch. 3), I would welcome it; I cannot now see that it could be.

T15 *R.* I, 351A5–6: "for injustice is ignorance – no one could still not know this (οὐδεὶς ἂν ἔτι τοῦτο²⁵ ἀγνοήσειεν)."

– that is to say, now everyone would know it: *a fortiori*, so would Socrates.

There are two more passages where Socrates lets on that he has knowledge without actually saying so. The first comes late in the *Gorgias*, when the fight against Callicles has been won and Socrates is engaged in mopping-up operations. He tells a parable. A sea-captain who has brought his passengers safe to port after a perilous journey muses on whether or not he did them a good turn by bringing them back alive. His thoughts take a Socratic turn. He reasons that if one of them had been suffering from "a grave and incurable" physical ailment, to him safe return would have been no boon. Nor would it, the captain reflects, to one afflicted with an equally grievous illness of the soul "which is so much more precious than the body." Then Socrates adds:

T16 *G.* 512B1–2: "He *knows* that for a wicked man it is better not to live, for he must needs live ill."

This sea-captain is Socrates' creature. His thought and reasonings are what Socrates says they are.²⁶ So for Socrates to say that the sea-captain knows that for an incurably wicked man death would be better than life is as good as saying that he, Socrates, knows this.

This same admission is made in the *Crito*, where we meet the same doctrine that just as life would not be worth living in a disease-ravaged, ruined body, so neither would it be worth living with a comparably damaged soul. Here this is expounded by Socrates himself *in propria persona* – from 47D7 to 48A3 he speaks in direct discourse – and simultaneously imputed to a mysterious figure who is described only as "the one, if there is one, who knows" (*Cr.* 47D1–2):

T17 48A5–7: "About the just and the unjust, O best of men, we should consider not what the many but what the man who knows shall say to us – that single man and the truth."

---

²⁵ I take the referent to be the immediately preceding clause, ἐπειδήπερ ἐστὶν ἀμαθία ἡ ἀδικία, which follows directly from the long argument at 348C2–350C11, whose conclusion was asserted categorically (ἀναπέφανται, 350C10) and is now regarded as agreed (διωμολογησάμεθα, 350D4).

²⁶ And most certainly believes to be true: cf. *G* 505A–B and *Cr.* 47D–E, where Socrates speaks directly, without resort to a notional mouthpiece.

Who is this man? Like the sea-captain of the first parable he is a construct of the argument. Socrates would have no ground for imputing knowledge about anything to either figure unless he were convinced that he himself had that knowledge. If he did not believe *he* knows what he says *they* know, his saying that they do would be a fraud.

Thus Socrates' disavowal of knowledge is a paradox. He makes it frequently, explicitly, emphatically: and its sincerity cannot be doubted, for what he tells others he also tells himself in the inmost privacy of self-scrutiny where he is not preparing a face to meet the faces he will meet but facing up to what he is. But when we go through our texts dispassionately, without initial *parti pris*, we see first (T9, T10) that knowledge, not true belief, is what he keeps searching for, and then, if we keep looking as carefully and imaginatively as we should, we can satisfy ourselves that Socrates is himself convinced that he has found what he has been looking for: knowledge of moral truth he avows openly in T11, programmatically in T12, by clear implication in T13 and T15, through notional proxies in T16 and T17. Can we make sense of this behavior? I want to argue that we can.

II

Let us reflect on our own use of the terms "know" and "knowledge." That they are all-purpose words, used to mean quite different things in different contexts, is a commonplace in present-day philosophy. But there is one aspect of this commonplace which is seldom noticed and when first noticed may even look like a paradox: there are times when we readily say, in a given context, that we know something, while in a sufficiently different context we would be reluctant to say we know it and might even prefer to deny that we do, and this without any sense of having contradicted ourselves thereby. Consider the proposition, "Very heavy smoking is a cause of cancer." Ordinarily I would have no hesitation in saying that I know this, though I have not researched the subject and have not tried to learn even the half of what could be learned from those who have. Now suppose that I am challenged, "But *do* you know it?" Sensing the shift to the stronger criteria for "knowing" the questioner has in view, I might then freely confess that I don't, adding perhaps, "If you want to talk to someone who does, ask N." – a renowned medical physiologist who has been researching the problem for years. By saying in this context, "He knows, I don't," I would not be implying that I had made a mistake when I had previously said I did know – that what I should have said instead is that all I had was a true belief. The conviction on whose strength I had acted when I gave up smoking years ago had not been just a true belief. I had reasons for it – imperfect ones, to be sure, which would not have been nearly good enough for a research scientist: in his case it would be a disgrace to say *he* knows on reasons no better than those. But for me those reasons were, and still are, good enough "for all practical purposes"; on the strength of those admittedly imperfect reasons I had made one of the *wisest* decisions of my life.

I submit that along roughly similar lines – the parallel is meant to be suggestive, not exact – we may look for our best explanation for the extraordinary fact that, without evincing any sense of inconsistency or even strain, Socrates can deny, and does habitually deny, that he has knowledge while being well aware that he does have it. To resolve the paradox we need only suppose that he is making a dual use of his words for knowing. When declaring that he knows absolutely nothing he is referring to that very strong sense in which philosophers had used them before and would go on using them long after – where one says one knows only when one is claiming certainty. This would leave him free to admit that he does have moral knowledge in a radically weaker sense – the one required by his own maverick method of philosophical inquiry, the elenchus. This is the hypothesis to which I referred at the start. I shall explain it further in the present section and shall proceed to argue for it in detail in the next.

I start with a passage that gives good insight into the conception of knowledge acceptable to Greek philosophers around this time:

T18 *R.* v, 477E: Socrates: "Not long ago you agreed that knowledge and belief are not the same." Glaucon: "How could any man of sense identify that which is infallible (ἀναμάρτητον) with that which is not infallible?" Socrates: "You are right."

Is Plato[27] really saying that to qualify as knowledge a cognitive state must possess infallibility? That is how his own word comes through all the standard translations. But considering how strong a view we would be imputing to him if we were really to understand him to be saying that this is what distinguishes knowledge from true belief, let us make sure that we are not doing so on the strength of a tendentious translation. The Greek word could be used to mean not "inerrable" (that which cannot be in error), but only "inerrant" (that which is not in error). We can see Plato elsewhere using the word in each of these ways: in the latter, when Theaetetus tells Socrates, in striking contrast to what Glaucon had told him in our present text, that true belief (δοξάζειν ἀληθῆ) is ἀναμάρτητον[28] – not in error (*Tht.* 200E); in the former, when Socrates asks Thrasymachus if rulers are ἀναμάρτητοι – incapable of error (*R.* 1, 339C1).[29] Can we be sure that the latter, not the former, is the way ἀναμάρτητον is being used in our present text? We can. Plato is laying down a criterion for distinguishing knowledge from belief as such – hence from true, no less than false, belief. Inerrancy could not serve this purpose: if a belief is true, it is no less inerrant than is knowledge.[30] "Infallible" then must be what Plato means. So he is maintaining that we know that *P* is true only when we possess the very highest degree of certainty concerning the truth of *P*.

On first hearing, this notion is forbiddingly intractable. One hardly knows how to come to grips with a conception which endows secular knowledge with infallible certainty. We can make better

---

[27] The reader may be reminded that I take the "Socrates" of Plato's middle dialogues to be a mouthpiece for what Plato thinks at the time of writing, when he is no longer recreating his teacher's philosophizing (*Socrates*, ch. 2, and cf. n. 13 *sub fin.*).

[28] Correctly translated "free of mistakes" by McDowell, 1973. What Theaetetus means we can see from the immediate follow-up, "and all that results from it is admirable and good," which as McDowell observes *ad loc.*: "is best understood in the light of *Meno* 96D5–97C11," i.e. that for the right guidance of action true belief is as good as knowledge.

[29] This has to be the sense if Thrasymachus is to sustain his definition of "justice" as "the interest of 'the stronger' " *and* maintain that to obey the "stronger" is (always) just (339B7–8). For given the latter, then, were the ruler (*qua* "stronger") to issue a mistaken order, to obey it would be just, yet also unjust, since it commands the doing something contrary to the interest of the "stronger." To avoid this contradiction Thrasymachus' definition of "justice" must be buttressed up by the assumption that *qua* "stronger" the ruler is *incapable of error*, infallible.

[30] When the ambiguity is thus resolved there is, obviously, no contradiction in Plato's saying in T18 that true belief is not ἀναμάρτητον and saying in *Tht.* 200E that it is.

progress by outflanking the position, explaining why the conception which is being denied makes excellent sense – is indeed the one we live by all the time. What would be meant by saying that our everyday knowledge is fallible? Without assaying any deep epistemology, it will suffice for present purposes to hold that one has fallible knowledge that *P* is true if the following conditions are fulfilled:

1   One believes *P* on evidence *Q*;
2   *P* is true and *Q* is true;
3   *Q* is reasonable evidence for *P*;
4   But *Q* does not entail *P*. *Q* could be true and *P* false.[31]

Let "*P*" stand for "I locked the door when I left the house this morning." Do I know this? I would not hesitate to say so. Is my claim to know it infallible? Obviously not. Why not? Because the evidence, *Q*, does not entail the truth of *P*.

Let *Q* be, as is often the case, just my memory of having turned the key in the lock as I went out of the door. The truth of *Q*[32] certainly does not entail that of *P*: my memory, usually reliable, goes wrong at times. This could be one of those times. Is it then reasonable to believe *P* on evidence as insecure as that? Yes, entirely reasonable. For suppose the contrary. Suppose that I insisted on stronger evidence. I could get it, for example, by phoning a neighbor to try the door or, better still, by rushing back to check the door myself. Would this be a reasonable thing to do? It would not: the benefit of the strengthened evidence would not be worth its cost: there is greater utility in living with the risk that *P* might be mistaken than in going to the trouble it would take to reduce the insecurity of its evidential base. There are circumstances when it *would* be reasonable to do that. Suppose there had been many burglaries

---

[31] I have laid down sufficient conditions for fallible knowledge: where "knowledge" = "justified true belief," "fallible knowledge" = "fallibly justified true belief," i.e. true belief whose justification falls short of certainty because it rests on evidence which constitutes reasonable grounds for the belief but does not guarantee its truth. In saying that such knowledge is fallible one is not saying that one may be mistaken in believing what one knows to be true (which would be nonsense: "I know *P*" entails "*P* is true," as Socrates recognized [*G*. 454D]), but only that one may be mistaken in claiming to know this, i.e. in claiming that one has reasonable evidence for that belief and that the belief is true.
[32] I.e. the fact that I do have this memory, which may, or may not, be veridical.

in my neighborhood and that a priceless Picasso was hanging in the living room in plain view of anyone entering the house. Then it would be reasonable to go to enormous trouble to raise my certainty that the door was locked. But since nothing much is in jeopardy if *P* is false, I am well content to claim that I know *P* on nothing better than my recollection. If I were not content to live with such deflation of the demands for certainty I would, quite literally, go mad: I would join the complusive hand-washer, who will not accept the fact that he has scrubbed his hands with hisofex just ten minutes ago as a good reason for believing that they are now free from deleterious germs. The willingness to live with fallible knowledge is built into the human condition. Only a god could do without it. Only a crazy man would want to.

We can now confront the alternative conception of knowledge that led a great philosopher to accept infallibility as its hallmark. Clearly, he did not mean to cover cases like the ones in my example. These he would dismiss as kitchen-stuff. His paradigm cases would be precisely those in which it is plausible to claim that the security-gap between *Q* and *P* cannot arise. In Aristotle these may be the ones where in his view no *Q* distinct from *P* is required – propositions which, as he puts it, "are known through themselves":

T19 Aristotle, *Pr. An.* 64b34–6: "It is of the nature of some things to be known through themselves; of other things to be known through things other than themselves."

All of the first principles of a science (its ἐπιστημονικαὶ ἀρχαί) are of this sort: propositions "true and primary, which produce conviction not through other things but through themselves" (*Top.* 100b18–19). For Aristotle just to understand (or "think," νοεῖν) such propositions is to be satisfied of their truth:

T20 Aristotle, *Metaph.* 1051b31–1052a1: "About such things it is impossible to be deceived: we either think them or not (ἀλλ᾽ ἢ νοεῖν ἢ μή) ... to think them is [to possess] the truth."[33]

---

[33] Aristotle is not appealing to self-evidence as a psychological state, i.e. to the feeling of certainty, but to insight – that understanding of essence which he takes to be encapsulated in the first principles of an axiomatized science (cf. the quotation from Burnyeat in the next note *sub fin.*) Though "self-evidence" is a close counterpart of Aristotle's phrase "know δι᾽ αὐτό" (from which our term "self-evident" seems to derive *via* the Latin *per se notum*), it may be best to avoid it lest it suggest a psychological process which Aristotle does not have in view.

If we start with propositions of this sort, making them the "first principles" (*archai*) of our demonstrations, and move beyond them only by steps of necessary inference, every proposition in the sequence will satisfy the infallibility criterion: for any *P* in that ordered system – be it one of its "immediate" first principles or one of the necessary derivations therefrom – the claim that *P* is true could go wrong only if we fail to understand what we are saying or what follows necessarily from it. Here every *P*, as Aristotle likes to emphasize, is a necessary statement:

T21 Aristotle, *Post. An.* 71b15–16: "If something is the object of unqualified knowledge, it is impossible for it to be otherwise (τοῦτ' ἀδύνατον ἄλλως ἔχειν),"[34]

Statements of this sort no argument could induce us to take back:

T22 Aristotle, *Post. An.* 72b3–4: "He who has unqualified knowledge must be immovable by persuasion (ἀμετάπειστον εἶναι)."

In Plato too the essentials of this conception of knowledge are maintained, though reached by a different route, for Plato's attitude to mathematics, the model science of the age, is so different.[35] For Aristotle the first principles of that science are self-certifying. Not so for Plato, who regards the axiom-sets of geometry and number-theory as mere "hypotheses" and the mathematician as "dreaming about reality" so long as his demonstrations have no greater security at their base.[36] That is where Plato's dialectician must take over, treating the primitives of mathematics as mere "stepping-stones" and "springboards" to "the first principle of all,"[37] which is itself

---

[34] Cf. Burnyeat, 1981: 111: "To understand a theorem you must understand [that] ... it is necessary because it is demonstrable from prior principles which are themselves necessary ... because they are *per se* predications expressing a definitional connection (*Pr. An.* 74b5–12 with 1,4). What is required is a predication *AaB* where either *A* belongs in the definition of *B* or *B* belongs in the definition of *A*."

[35] I have in view the definitive position in the middle books of the *Republic*: not the transitional one displayed in the *M.*, where he borrows from the geometricians the "hypothetical method of investigation" (ἐξ ὑποθέσεως σκοπεῖσθαι, 86E), offers no critique of mathematics, and draws the distinction between knowledge and true belief (97E–98A) without reference to the "unhypothesized first principle" of the *Republic* (VI, 510B7, 511B6) and without appeal to an ontology of eternal Forms.

[36] "We see that they are dreaming about being and cannot have a wide-awake vision of it so long as using hypotheses they leave them unshaken, unable to give an account of them" (*R.* VII, 533B8–C3). Contrast the description of the same people – unphilosophical mathematicians – in the *Euthydemus*, which, in common with most scholars, I have been dating before the *Meno*: "they discover being" (τὰ ὄντα ἀνευρίσκουσιν, 290C3).

[37] τὴν τοῦ παντὸς ἀρχήν, *R.* VI, 511B6–7.

certain and confers certainty on everything grounded on it.[38] So for Plato too, as for Aristotle, knowledge consists of propositions which are "secure and unshakable" (*Ti* 29B7) and differs from true opinion in its "unmovability" by countervailing argument:

T23 Plato, *Ti.* 51E4: "[Knowledge] is immovable by persuasion, while [true belief] can be changed by persuasion."

And for him too, as for Aristotle, if *P* is known to be true, then *P* is necessarily true: his whole epistemology is built on the restriction of what is known to what is necessarily true. This is the unavoidable consequence of his cardinal metaphysical doctrine that the subject matter of *bona fide* knowledge consists exclusively of eternal forms – entities, all of whose properties, locked into their definitions, are as immune to contingency as are the truths of logic and mathematics.

In taking this position Plato and Aristotle were not disporting eccentric views. They felt they were articulating the philosophical consensus of their age. Says Aristotle:

T24 *N.E.* 1139b19–21: "We all believe that what we know could not be otherwise (μηδ' ἐνδέχεσθαι ἄλλως ἔχειν)."

That Plato too speaks for what he takes to be a consensus shows in the way he brings up the infallibility criterion in the snatch of the dialogue quoted above. If he had anticipated resistance he would have had Socrates introduce it, Glaucon demur, and Socrates argue down Glaucon's objection. What he does instead is to have Glaucon state it, and Socrates accept it unquestioningly. The mode of presentation is that of a truth so obvious that no reasonable reader could be expected to gainsay it.

The antecedents of this view can be discerned a generation or more before Socrates, in the dawn of metaphysics in Greece, when epistemology, still in its infancy, is not yet a fully articulated discipline and its doctrines are set forth in oracular prose (as in Heraclitus) or in poetic form (as in Parmenides and Empedocles). To

---

[38] I take this to be the implication of the dialectician's going ἐπ' αὐτὴν τὴν ἀρχὴν ἵνα βεβαιώσηται, *R.* VII, 533C–D: so long as one does what mathematicians do, proving their theorems from primitives which are themselves ungrounded, all one can claim is that one's system has internal consistency, and only "by force of habit" can this be called "knowledge" (533D): *bona fide* knowledge is reached when, and only when, "doing away with hypotheses, one reaches the first principle to find certainty there."

illustrate from Parmenides: his implicit acceptance of indubitable certainty as the prerogative of the philosopher's knowledge shows up in the fictional guise of divine revelation in which he presents his metaphysical (and even his physical) system. His treatise is the notional discourse of a goddess who reveals to him "the unshaken heart of well-rounded truth" (ἀληθείης εὐκυκλέος³⁹ ἀτρεμὲς ἦτορ, B1, 29), i.e. a doctrine that is undisturbable by objections ("unshaken") and systematically complete ("well-rounded"). The appeal is throughout to critical reason, not to faith; the goddess does not say "Close your eyes and believe," but "Open your mind and attend to the 'strife-encompassed refutation'⁴⁰ I offer." But the hierophantic trappings of the argument attest the certainty its author attaches to its conclusion. Even considerably later, in the materialist, Democritus, Socrates' contemporary, the conviction that genuine knowledge must possess certainty persists. Unlike his predecessors, Democritus has the gravest misgivings that such knowledge can be attained. He even seems to deny that it can:

T25 Democritus, fr. B117 (Diels–Kranz): "In reality we know nothing, for truth is in the depths."

But this despairing conclusion does not express rejection of the dogma that knowledge entails certainty. It attests the dogma. Had Democritus glimpsed the possibility of fallible knowledge, he could not have drawn such a conclusion from his conviction that:

T26 Democritus, fr. B9 (Diels–Kranz): "... in reality we know nothing with certainty (ἡμεῖς δὲ τῷ μὲν ἐόντι οὐδὲν ἀτρεκὲς συνίεμεν)."

From "We know nothing with certainty" he could not have inferred "In reality we know nothing" except on the tacit premise "In reality we know only what we know with certainty."

I shall use "knowledge_C" to designate knowledge so conceived, using the subscript as a reminder that infallible certainty was its hallmark. Now whatever Socrates might be willing to say he *knows* in the domain of ethics would have to be knowledge reached and tested through his own personal method of inquiry, the elenchus;

---

³⁹ I follow the latest editor, M. Schofield (in Kirk, Raven, and Schofield, 1983): a difficult decision in favor of εὐκυκλέος, though the alternative reading, εὐπειθέος, has strong attestation, and is accepted by some editors.
⁴⁰ I follow Schofield's translation of πολύδηριν ἔλεγχον, *op. cit*, p. 248.

this is his only method of searching for moral truth.[41] So when he avows knowledge – as we have seen he does, rarely, but unmistakably – the content of that knowledge must be propositions he thinks elenctically justifiable.[42] I shall, therefore, call it "elenctic knowledge," abbreviating to "knowledge$_E$."

Socrates could not have expected his knowledge$_E$ to meet the fantastically strong standards of knowledge$_C$. No great argument should be needed to show this. In elenctic inquiry nothing is ever "known through itself" but only "through other things" and there is always a security gap between the Socratic thesis and its supporting reasons. And the general reason Socrates has for the truth of any particular thesis of his is that it is elenctically viable: it can be maintained consistently in elenctic argument, while its denial cannot. This, in the last analysis, is the Q for every proposition, P, in the domain of ethics which Socrates claims to know; his reason in each case is, at bottom, twofold:

Q[a] P is entailed by beliefs held by anyone who denies it;
Q[b]   *not-P* is not entailed by beliefs held by Socrates who affirms P.

The claim is trebly insecure. For, to begin with, even if Q[a] were true, all it would prove is that Socrates' interlocutors happen to have beliefs which, unbeknown to themselves, entail the Socratic thesis which they dispute – a very remarkable fact indeed, if fact it is, but what would it show? It could not begin to show that those beliefs are true.[43] But *is* Q[a] true? What could be Socrates' evidence for that?

---

[41] *Pace* Irwin, 1977: 37 and 39; cf. ch. 1, n. 51, above.
[42] This is what Socrates would understand by saying he "knows" the moral truth in T11 above, since the only reason he could offer is that the claim is justifiable by elenctic argument. So too by saying at T12 he "knows well" that the premises on which he can get Callicles to agree are true: they are propositions he would stand ready to justify by elenctic argument if Callicles were to dispute their truth. This is evidently the sense of "you know" at T13, i.e. it has been demonstrated to you by elenctic argument. So too *mutatis mutandis* at T15, T16, T17. And see the comment on T28[b] (=T6) in n. 47 below.
[43] To show this, Q[a] would have to be strengthened to:

Q[A] P is entailed by *true* beliefs held by anyone who denies it

which is equivalent to the proposition I formulated more fully in ch. 1 (p. 25) above as assumption [A] (the "tremendous" assumption):

A Anyone who ever has a false moral belief will always have at the same time true beliefs entailing its negation.

Simply his own experience in elenctic practice. What would that prove? Suppose $Q[a]$ had turned out true in a thousand elenchi; it might still turn out false in the thousand-and-first. And is $Q[b]$ true? Can the elenchus prove it true? Elenchus is not a computer into which sets of propositions can be fed to have their consistency checked with mechanical accuracy. It is a human process, a contest, whose outcome is drastically affected by the skill and drive of the contestants. So if Socrates wins all the arguments this may only show that he is the better debater. It could not show that there is no inconsistency within his own set of beliefs – only that, if there is, no opponent has managed to spot it.

Socrates could not have been unaware of this uncertainty, built into his instrument of research, which infects all its findings. That he is not so blind shows up in remarks he makes from time to time. So, for example, in this aside to Critias:

T27 *Ch.* 166c7–d4: How could you think that I would refute you for any reason but the one for which I would refute myself, fearing lest I might inadvertently think I know something when I don't know it? And this, I say, is what I am doing now, examining the argument chiefly for my own sake, though no doubt also for the sake of my friends.

Since by "to know" Socrates here is referring directly to what he seeks to achieve by elenctic inquiry, the fear he is voicing is that he might think true theses which have fared well in past elenctic inquiry but are in fact false. In saying that this fear fuels his elenctic searching he reveals his haunting sense of the insecurity of knowledge$_E$ – his awareness that in respect of certainty it is the diametrical opposite of knowledge$_C$.

There is a further respect in which Socratic knowledge is poles

---

The other assumption I gave Socrates in ch. 1 (p. 28) is:

B   The set of moral beliefs held by Socrates at any given time is consistent.

B is equivalent to $Q[b]$ above. I have scaled down A to $Q[a]$ in response to helpful criticism from my friends, Thomas Brickhouse and Nicholas Smith, 1984: 185ff., and 187–90. It is now clear to me that inductive evidence (extrapolation from past experience in elenctic practice) which is available to Socrates for $Q[b]$ is not available to him for $Q[A]$: all he can hope to justify from that source is, at most $Q[b]$ is not available to him for $Q[A]$: all he can hope to justify from that source is, at most $Q[a]$. $Q[A]$, thus unsupported and unsupportable within the elenctic dialogues, must await the metaphysical grounding it will be given by Plato in the *Meno*: transmigration and the theory of recollection ensure that true beliefs entailing the negation of every false belief are innate in the soul.

apart from knowledge$_C$: it is full of gaps, unanswered questions; it is surrounded and invaded by unresolved perplexity. But this does not trouble Socrates. He does not find it debilitating, but exhilarating, as well he may, for what he needs to make his method work is not completeness but consistency within that set of elenctically testable beliefs which constitute his knowledge$_E$. At no time does his method require of him that he produce himself the answers to the questions his interlocutors fail to find. The task it sets him is to refute bogus ones, and this he does by eliciting from them the beliefs which generate the negation of their false answers. So if an inquiry should run into *aporia*, he can reckon the exercise not failure but incomplete success. Nothing has transpired to show that the unfound answer is unfindable, nor yet to invalidate the fragmentary truths unearthed along the way and shake his claim that in their case he does have knowledge$_E$.[44]

So this is the hypothesis: in the domain of morals – the one to which all of his inquiries are confined – when he says he knows something he is referring to knowledge$_E$; when he says he is not aware of knowing anything – absolutely anything, "great or small" (T7) – he refers to knowledge$_C$; when he says he has no knowledge of a particular topic he may mean *either* that in this case, as in all others, he has no knowledge$_C$ and does not look for any *or* that what he lacks on that topic is knowledge$_E$, which, with good luck, he might still reach by further searching.

III

If this hypothesis were true it would explain the most perplexing feature of Socrates' epistemic stance.[45] It would show how he could,

---

[44] Scrutiny of any of the aporetic dialogues should satisfy anyone that en route to the eventual *aporia* Socrates produces elenctic justification of important theses whose truth is unaffected by the eventual failure to find the answer to the "What is the *F*?" question.

[45] And the most distinctive – unparalleled in the whole of the philosophical literature of the West (no other major philosopher ever puts himself in the position of saying "I have proved, but do not know, that *p* is true"); unparalleled also in any post-elenctic Platonic dialogue, even the *Theaetetus*, where Plato's Socrates simulates Socratic ignorance in its most extreme form ("I question others but make no assertion about anything myself [cf. T3 above], for there is no wisdom in me" [150c5–6]): even there Plato never puts Socrates in the position of saying he doesn't know a proposition for which he has produced un-contested, apparently conclusive, proof; thus, when Socrates reaches the conclusion that knowledge is to be found not in sense-perception but "in what goes on when the soul

and should, have wanted to say that *after he had proved* his theses true he still did not "know" if they are true. We see him doing so in the case of that central doctrine of his for which he does battle in the *Gorgias*, first against Polus and then, at greater length and from different premises, against Callicles – that to suffer injustice is always better than to do it:[46]

T28 *G.* 508E6–509A5: [a]"... these things have been clamped down and bound by arguments of iron and adamant ... "

[b] (= T6 above) "But as for me my position is always the same: I do not know how these things are."

At [a] Socrates implies that he has proved his doctrine true: earlier on, in his argument against Polus, he had not hesitated to *say* he had:

T29 *G.* 479E8: "Has it not been proved that what was asserted [by myself] is true?"

Is Socrates then welshing in part [b] of T28 on what he has just said to Callicles in its part [a] and more explicitly to Polus in T29? Is he retracting his claim to have proved – and thus shown that he knows – that his doctrine is true? On the proposed hypothesis this quandary does not arise; for what he disclaims in T28[b] and, implicitly, claims in T28[a] and T29 are altogether different things: implying that he has knowledge$_E$,[47] he denies that he has knowledge$_C$.[48]

He has made the same disclaimer of knowledge$_C$ a little earlier in

---

occupies itself by itself with being" (*Tht.* 187A4–6), he is not made to reiterate his total disavowal of knowledge; he does not turn around and say he doesn't know what, to all appearance, he has just shown that he has come to know.

[46] A corollary of his rejection of the *lex talionis* which he and others feel separates him irreconcilably from the established morality: cf. *Cr.* 49C10–D5 with *G.* 481C1–4.

[47] That this is all he meant to claim in T29 can be inferred from the fact that elenctic argument was all he has offered by way of support for the theses he had "proved" true. That this is what he means at T28 is even clearer: to continue the citation (509A5–7), "but of all those I have encountered, none has proved capable of speaking otherwise without making himself ridiculous [i.e. by being shown to have beliefs which contradict his assertion], as happened just now." He is saying: the only proof I can offer for my doctrine is that all those who have opposed it in elenctic argument have been defeated in that argument. Since that result does not entail the truth of his doctrine but does constitute, in his view, reasonable evidence for it, he is perfectly justified in disclaiming knowledge$_C$ and claiming knowledge$_E$ of its truth, as he does by implication, at T16 above, where his proxy, the philosophical sea-captain, "knows" (= knows$_E$) that persistent wrongdoing would be so ruinous to one's happiness that the wrongdoer would be better off dead than alive.

[48] Straining to catch this sense Robin slips into over-translation: οὐκ οἶδα at *G.* 509A5 he renders "*je ne sais pas d'une science certaine.*"

the *Gorgias,* in a context where he availed himself of both the opposing uses of "know" within a single paragraph of Plato's text:

T30 *G.* 505E4–506A4: "... We should all be contentiously eager to know
[= know$_E$]⁴⁹ what is true and what is false about the things we discuss ... [So]
if it appears to any of you that what I admit to myself is not the truth, you must
interrupt and refute me. For I do not assert what I assert as one who knows
[= knows$_C$] ... "

When the critical terms are disambiguated in this way we can see
not only what Socrates means to say but why he should want to say
it at this juncture when it is clear to everyone that he has won the
debate. He says in the *Apology* (23A3–5) that those who witness his
dialectical victories would think him wise [= wise$_C$] in those things
in which he refutes others – a natural enough impression they might
derive from seeing him maintain over and over again his record as
undefeated champion of the elenchus-ring. So in our present passage
in the *Gorgias,* marking a moment at which he has given a stunning
demonstration that he does have knowledge$_E$ of the truth of his
theses, he has special reason to warn his hearers that he does not
have knowledge$_C$, thereby underlining the sincerity and urgency for
his desire to entertain objections: if he allowed his hearers to believe
that he was speaking as one who has knowledge$_C$ his professed interest in hearing criticism would ring hollow.

Similarly we could go through all the texts in Plato's elenctic
dialogues in which "know," "knowledge," "wise," "wisdom" occur
– all of those I cited earlier and all those others I have had no
occasion to cite – resolving their ambiguities in the same way. So
understood, all of those statements will make sense. Socrates will
never be contradicting himself by saying, or implying, that he both
has and hasn't knowledge, for he will not be saying, or implying,
that he does and doesn't have knowledge$_E$ or that he does and
doesn't have knowledge$_C$, but only that he does have knowledge$_E$
and does not have knowledge$_C$. Thus his avowal of ignorance will
never generate practical inconsistency or doctrinal incoherence.
When he tells the interlocutor that he has no knowledge he will not
be violating the "say what you believe" rule of elenctic debate, for

---

⁴⁹ That this is the sort of knowledge to which he is referring is clear from the fact that elenctic
   argument is the method by which it is being sought; cf. T26 above.

he will not be feigning ignorance: he does believe with full conviction, with utter sincerity, that he has no knowledge$_C$.[50] Nor will he be endangering his doctrine that "Virtue is knowledge" when this is read, as it should be, "Virtue is knowledge$_E$."

Moreover, the hypothesis explains why Socrates should make, not the avowal of knowledge$_E$, but the disavowal of knowledge$_C$ his front before the world, his epistemic manifesto as it were: only once, it will be remembered (T11 above), does he say in so many words that he knows a moral truth. In all the other texts that go the same way he avows knowledge by indirection, as if, after shouting "I don't know" he would only whisper "and yet I do." The hypothesis motivates this asymmetry. If knowledge$_C$ is what everyone expects of you as a philosopher and you are convinced that you have none of it, not a smidgin of it, you would naturally have reason to advertise your ignorance and admit your knowledge inconspicuously, almost furtively.

So far the hypothesis earns its salt. But two big questions still remain. The first arises over the fact that when Socrates heard that report from Delphi he was *surprised*. Why so, on this hypothesis?[51] Why should he not have thought the tribute well deserved? Not all of his elenctic searches had failed. On some absolutely fundamental things he had struck gold. He had come to know – know$_E$ – things which "to know is noblest, not to know most base: who is happy and who is not."[52] Why then should he feel perplexed at the oracle's declaration that no man was wiser than himself? In none of the texts I have reviewed is there even a glimmer of the answer. Fortunately there are two more, both of them from the context of the oracle story and its aftermath: when undertaking to explain away his public image as "wise man," Socrates confesses that on this score the public

---

[50] Since the elenchus is Socrates' sole access to moral knowledge.

[51] I shall waste no time on the easy answer "because he thought there would be others with much higher credentials": it founders on the brilliant triumphs Socrates scores (e.g. in the *Pr.* where he is still *young* [314B, 317C, 361E]) over those most highly reputed for their "wisdom" throughout Greece. If Chaerephon had not expected some such answer as the one he got he would not have asked his question. So *he* could not have been greatly surprised. Why should Socrates? (*Pace* Burnet's gloss on *Ap.* 21A5, we get no light on our question from the report in Diogenes Laertius [2.65] that Aristippus had been drawn to Athens from far-off Cyrene "by Socrates' fame": Diogenes' authority is excellent [Aeschines of Sphettus], but he gives no indication of the relative time-frames.)

[52] T10, abbreviated.

had not been altogether wrong:

T31 *Ap.* 20D6–E2: "I came by this reputation, O Athenians, only by a sort of wisdom (διὰ σοφίαν τινά). What sort of wisdom? Exactly that sort which is, no doubt (ἴσως), human wisdom (ἀνθρωπίνη σοφία). It looks as though (κινδυνεύω) in this I am really wise (τῷ ὄντι ... σοφός). But those of whom I spoke just now[53] are wise in a wisdom that is more than human (μείζω τινὰ ἢ κατ' ἄνθρωπον σοφίαν) – I don't know how else to speak of it (ἢ οὐκ ἔχω τί λέγω)."

Here Socrates admits in so many words what I have been hypothesizing all along: that he can use "wisdom" (and "knowledge") to refer to either of two radically different cognitive achievements, one of which Socrates dares claim to have while disclaiming the other. And that this "human wisdom" of his, which he openly avows here, could only be knowledge$_E$ follows from the fact that the elenchus had been his only way of seeking it. He goes on to offer Delphic certification of his claim to have such knowledge:

T32 *Ap.* 23A5–B4: "It looks as though the god is really wise and that what he is saying in this oracle is this: human wisdom is worth little or nothing. By referring to this 'Socrates' he seems to be using my name as an example, as if he were saying, 'That one of you, O men, is wisest, who, like Socrates, has understood that in relation to wisdom he is truly worthless (οὐδενὸς ἄξιός ἐστι τῇ ἀληθείᾳ πρὸς σοφίαν).'"

Now he is denigrating his "human wisdom" – saying that in comparison with true wisdom, that of the god who "is really wise", his own is worthless. Why so? Isn't this our riddle all over again? If "the unexamined life is not worth living by man" (*Ap.* 38A5–6) and the elenchus is its examining, why shouldn't Socrates think the knowledge that issues from it is man's most precious possession? Why then should he be saying that it is "worth little or nothing"? Conversely, shouldn't he be debunking the alternative which, by his own description of it, is beyond man's reach, denouncing it as a will-o'-the-wisp, a mirage, product of the extravagant aspirations of deluded metaphysicians and word-happy sophists?

If Socrates had been an epistemologist this, surely, would be the line he would have had to take. His commitment to the elenctic method would have left him no other choice: it would have called

---

[53] Natural philosophers (18B–19D7) and sophists (19D8–20C3): cf. σοφός at 19C6 and then again at 20A3.

for a head-on collision with the prevailing paradigm of infallible, unrevisable, "unpersuadable" grasp of necessary truths, and a reasoned defense of a new model of fallible, provisional, corrigible knowledge. But the Socrates of this paper is no epistemologist. He is a moralist pure and simple who practices moral inquiry but never inquires into the theory of moral inquiry.[54] He is as innocent of epistemology as of metaphysics. He is no Dewey, led to the renunciation of the quest for certainty[55] by an "instrumentalist logic," no Wittgenstein, impelled in that direction by a critique of language. Our Socrates lacks the conceptual machinery that would be needed to dismantle the established paradigm and erect a new one in its place. When he peers at the abyss that yawns between knowledge$_C$ and knowledge$_E$ he measures the distance not in analytic but in religious terms. He broods on it in the spirit of traditional piety which counsels mortals to "think mortal" – to keep within the limits of the human condition:

T33 Euripides, *Bacchae* 395–7: "Cleverness is not wisdom (τὸ σοφὸν δ' οὐ σοφία). And not to think mortal thoughts (τό τε μὴ θνητὰ φρονεῖν), is to see few days."

T34 Sophocles, *Trach.* 473: "Being mortal, you think mortal thoughts: you are not senseless (θνητήν, φρονοῦσαν θνητὰ κοὐκ ἀγνώμονα)."

In this, as in so many other ways, he is poles apart from both Plato and Aristotle. Their philosophic outreach willfully defies the limits of mortality. Transcendence of finitude is the heart of Platonic mysticism. In Aristotle too this faith lives, though rarely voiced. In the *Metaphysics*, calling this science, provocatively, "divine knowledge" (θείαν τῶν ἐπιστημῶν, 983a6–7), he protests the venerable dogma that "human nature is in bondage," denied that most sublime of cognitive achievements by the "jealousy of the gods." In the *Nicomachean Ethics* his rejection of the dogma is more defiant and explicit:

T35 *N.E.* 1177b31–4: "We should not heed those who counsel us that, being men, we should think human, and being mortals, we should think mortal. But we ought, so far as in us lies, to make ourselves immortal (καθ' ὅσον ἐνδέχεται ἀθανατίζειν), straining every nerve to live in accordance with the highest thing in us."

---

[54] For argument to this effect see ch. 1 above.
[55] "The Quest for Certainty" had been the title of John Dewey's Gifford Lectures.

Socrates too strains every nerve to live in accordance with the highest thing in us. But this he takes to be elenctic reason – a poor thing, but man's own. Resigned to think human, he thinks with all his might: with the zest, tenacity, honesty, and daring of Socratic elenchus.

Now, I suggest, we can understand why Socrates is startled by Delphi's accolade. He can hardly bring himself to believe that his own understanding of the good life, chancy, patchy, provisional, perpetually self-questioning, endlessly perplexed as it is, should have any value at all in the eyes of the god who enjoys the unshaken heart of well-rounded truth – the perfect security, the serene completeness of knowledge$_C$. So he goes out into the world, searching high and low for something better. The search fails. He is then left with the conviction he expresses in T32: low as his own moral insight must rank by the god's absolute standards, it is still superior to any alternative open to man and earns the god's praise because it is humble. Drained of all epistemic presumption, aware of his own ignorance, he is aware that he has no knowledge$_C$.

But there is a further question: if that is the point of his "I don't know" – the shortfall in certainty that afflicts man's cognitive achievements at their best – why didn't he say so? Why should he choose to signal it only through an unresolved ambiguity? The question concerns linguistic conventions. Would contemporary speech-patterns have tolerated so devious a form of communication? On this I could discourse at length. In Heraclitus, Sophocles, Euripides ambiguous utterance is a favorite form of pregnant speech. I must content myself with one example: T33, τὸ σοφὸν δ' οὐ σοφία. Since the articular neuter adjective is in Greek idiom precisely equivalent to the cognate abstract noun, what Euripides is saying, put into literal, unmanipulated, English, is just "Wisdom is not wisdom" – a blank self-contradiction at which translators balk: they can't swallow what is said in the Greek, so they doctor it up: "The world's wise are not wise" (Gilbert Murray); "Cleverness is not wisdom" (Dodds), and so forth. The Greek poet feels no such block. He flings his sentence at the audience, sure that no one in it will fail to catch on instantly, understanding τὸ σοφόν to refer to the μὴ θνητὰ φρονεῖν displayed in that brash, sneering, jeering, smartalecky ration-alism of Pentheus, the extreme opposite of "wisdom" in that other sense of the word represented by Teiresias – reverent acceptance of the ancestral faith whose rejection by Pentheus will spell his doom. Couldn't the poet have said this more plainly? Obviously he could. Who would suppose that to contrive a metrical equivalent of δει-νότης οὐ σοφία would have strained the resources of Euripidean prosody? But such gain in lucidity would have been poetic loss. If its paradox were defused where would be the wonder stirred in us by its oxymoron? Far better that he should have thrown the burden of disambiguation upon us.

If you say, "But Socrates is a philosopher, not a poet," I would remind you of what a maverick philosopher he is: a teacher who shuns didacticism, believing that moral truth has a dimension which eludes direct expression – a depth best revealed not by instruction but by provocation. For that purpose he invented the figure of speech which still bears his signature in the dictionaries. I did not gloss those entries on "Socratic irony" in *Webster's* and the *O.E.D.* when I cited them at the start. Had I done so I would have pointed out that they refer us only to the simplest uses of Socratic irony. Only in these is it a figure in which what is said is simply not what is meant. In Socrates' most powerful uses of it the irony is more com-plex: in these Socratic sayings what is said both is and isn't what is meant. So, certainly, in that other invention of his which still bears his name in common speech: Socratic teaching. He teaches saying he is not teaching. What he says is what he means if to teach is to impart to a learner truth already known to oneself. It is not what he means if to teach is to trigger in a learner an autonomous learning process. As instrument of Socratic teaching this irony is best left unresolved. Its purpose is not, as Kierkegaard would have it, to "deceive [the learner] into the truth."[56] It is to tease, mock, perplex him into seeking the truth. When the profession of ignorance is used for the same purpose its irony is likewise best left unexplained. In

---

[56] "One can deceive a person about the truth, and one can (remembering old Socrates) deceive a person into the truth. Indeed when a person is under an illusion, it is only by deceiving him that he can be brought into the truth" (quoted by Lowrie, 1938: 248).

telling himself he has no wisdom Socrates has no need to explain. In telling others he doesn't want to. He taunts them to ponder what he is hinting at by using words that do and don't say what he means.[57]

[57] I have presented here thoughts I have voiced in different forms on different occasions: in Gifford Lectures at St. Andrews in 1981; in Howison Lectures at Berkeley in 1984; in ad hoc lectures at the National Center for the Humanities in North Carolina in 1980 and 1981; in papers to seminars in Berkeley in 1983 and in Cambridge (England) in 1984. I have learned more than I could acknowledge from friends who have responded to these thoughts: principally Myles Burnyeat and Alan Code, from whom I have learned the most; but also Ian Kidd, Jonathan Lear, Geoffrey Lloyd, Alexander Nehamas, David Sedley, Dory Scaltsas, and Harold Tarrant. None of those I have thanked may be presumed to agree with views I have defended.

3

IS THE "SOCRATIC FALLACY" SOCRATIC?[1]

In the preceding chapter I argued for a hypothesis which, if true, would solve one of the standing puzzles in the history of Western philosophy: how a man who was anything but a skeptic – an earnest moralist, eager to propagate new, powerful moral doctrines of his own – betrayed no awareness of inconsistency in claiming that he had the strongest of reasons[2] for those doctrines and yet said he did not know if those doctrines were true. There is no inconsistency on the hypothesis that he is making a systematically dual use of his words for knowing, disavowing what philosophers had generally understood by "knowledge" at the time, namely, what I have called "knowledge$_C$," whose hallmark is infallible certainty, while avowing the highly fallible knowledge I have called "knowledge$_E$," where Socrates' claim to know p is simply the claim that p is elenctically viable, i.e., that if he were to pit it against its contradictory in elenctic argument it would prevail.

To say that this has been a standing puzzle of philosophical historiography may seem surprising, for it has not been treated as such in the copious literature on the subject. The reason for this, I believe, is simple: the relevant textual evidence has not been confronted. The evidence for one horn of the dilemma – for Socrates' disavowal of knowledge – is spread out so abundantly on the surface of Plato's

[1] This is, in substance, a lecture under the same title delivered at St. Andrews under the Gifford Trust in 1981 and at Berkeley as a Howison Lecture in 1984. I have made a number of changes in response to searching questions by the editor of *Ancient Philosophy*, whose help I acknowledge with thanks. It is a pleasure to refer to the paper by John Beversluis, 1987. Finding myself in close agreement with its views, I shall forgo cross-references to it.
[2] "Arguments of iron and adamant," *G.* 509A.

text that no one reading it even in a poor translation could miss it. But the evidence for the other horn surfaces explicitly only in that single text in the *Apology* (29B) whose singularity has damned it, as of course it would and should, were it not for that array of other texts[3] where Socrates does claim unambiguously, though only by implication, that he does have moral knowledge of the right way to live – knowledge, not just true belief. Once those further texts are noticed and given their full weight the paradox of Socrates' epistemic stance – declaring that he has no moral knowledge but nonetheless maintaining that he does – cries aloud for resolution. The hypothesis I have offered does just that. It does so consistently with all the evidence. If true, it dissolves the puzzle. Nonetheless the solution is a chancy one, for in the nature of the case it is not susceptible of direct confirmation. Its credentials are its explanatory value. In the present essay I shall pursue the argument for it one step further by extending its explanatory scope. I shall argue that, if the hypothesis were true, it would clear Socrates of a notorious fallacy[4] which has been charged against him so confidently that it has come to be regarded as his personal property, made to carry his very name, as it does in the present chapter's title.

Let me begin with its appearance in the *Lysis* – its first in Plato's corpus, as I shall be arguing. At the dialogue's very end, when the search for "What is the *philon* (dear)?" has dead-ended, Socrates remarks in the dialogue's last words:

T1 *Ly.* 223B: "We have made ourselves ridiculous – both you and also I, an old man. For as these people go away from here they will be saying that we are each others' friends (*philoi*) ..., yet what a friend (*philos*) is we have not proved able to discover."

The relation of the boys to each other and of Socrates to each is so straightforward a case of what is commonly understood by *philos* that what Socrates has just said is tantamount to claiming that if we don't know what a "friend" is, in the sense of possessing an elenctically viable definition of that term, we are not entitled to be-

---

[3] T13–T17 in ch. 2.
[4] Stretching "fallacy" to cover the "style of mistaken thinking" which Geach attributed to Socrates in 1966: cf. n. 6.

lieve that anyone is anyone's friend.[5] No extended argument should be needed to convince us that this view is false. Suppose we do not have, and never expect to have, a definition of "friend" or, say, of "beauty" or "humor" that meets Socrates' exacting standards or even looser ones. Would we see in this a serious objection to claiming to know that someone whose affection and trust we have enjoyed over the years is our friend; that Elizabeth Taylor in her prime was a beauty, while Eleanor Roosevelt was not; that there is humor in abundance in *Huckleberry Finn* and the *Pickwick Papers*, while there is all too little of it in the works of Theodore Dreiser and other lugubrious novelists? It is, therefore, understandable that this notion should have been branded a "fallacy" by Peter Geach in a famous paper.[6] For economy of reference I shall call it simply "proposition [G]" in Geach's honour, rephrasing it as follows:

[G]   If you do not know what the F[7] is, you will not know if you are predicating "F" correctly about *anything* whatever – you will not know if *anything* is F.

I have italicized "anything" because there lies the sting: the unqualified universality of the claim[8]. If all it were saying is that in the absence of a definition of the F there would be *some* reputed cases of it where we would be uncertain whether or not "F" is being correctly applied, the claim, though still a substantial one, would by no means be the outrageous one it presently is: it would not imply

---

[5] This is how I understand the import of this text: for $F = philos$, coming to know the answer to "What is the F?" is a necessary condition of being in a position to assert that the relation of X to Y is an instance of F; making this assertion without having fulfilled that condition makes one "ridiculous."

[6] 1966 (reprinted 1972). Though, as I shall be arguing, its main thesis is decidedly wrong, it has had a bracing effect on Socratic studies, having proved powerfully and fruitfully provocative. Much earlier Richard Robinson (1953: 51) had charged Socrates with a parallel error (the "priority of definition": to be discussed as "proposition [R]" below), but so indecisively that the charge elicited little response in the scholarly literature.

[7] The range of this variable is implicitly restricted to the moral predicates which are foci of Socratic investigation in Plato's earlier dialogues. Cf. n. 11 below.

[8] This should immediately disqualify as evidence of Socrates' acceptance of [G] certain texts in Plato's elenctic dialogues which have been mistakenly cited as evidence of it, in particular *Ch.* 176A–B (that it is nothing of the kind is clearly explained by Santas, 1972: 138) and *La.* 190C6 (cited as such by Irwin, 1977: 40, without comment and with no explanation of why we should take what Socrates says here – if we know virtue we should be able to tell what virtue is – as evidence that he accepts [G]).

that, pending discovery of a Socratic definition, *all* cases of the application of the concept, even perfectly straightforward, unproblematic, ones, have been unsettled.

Now is it really true that Plato wants his readers to think that the philosopher whose thought he recreates in his earliest dialogues had believed this extraordinary proposition? Geach took it for granted that it is. The assumption was challenged strongly by Gerasimos Santas[9] and Myles Burnyeat.[10] Absorbing what can be learned from their critiques of Geach, I now want to make a fresh start, reopening the problem from the bottom up. The bottom is the text I have just cited from the *Lysis* taken in conjunction with the next two I shall be citing directly, both of them from the *Hippias Major*, where the role of proposition [G] is much larger. Here, to come in view of it, we don't need, as in the *Lysis*, to await the dialogue's closing words. Here it serves to introduce, not just conclude, the fruitless search for the *F*:

T2 *HMa.* 286c–d: "The other day, as I was faulting certain things in some speeches, praising some as fine (*kala*),[11] censuring others as foul (*aischra*), someone threw me into a tizzy by questioning me most insolently, like this: 'Say, Socrates, how do you know which sort of things are fine or foul? For, come now, are you able to say what is the fine?'"

What Socrates' bullying critic is telling him is that if he has no answer to the question, "What is the fine?" he has no business judging that *anything* is fine. After repeated efforts, harebrained ones by Hippias, plausible but ineffectual ones by himself, Socrates finally gives up, cringing at the thought of returning empty-handed to face his merciless super-ego:

T3 *HMa.* 304d–e: "He will ask me if I am not ashamed to dare discuss fine practices when elenctic refutation makes it evident that I don't even know what on earth the fine itself is. 'So [a] how will you know,' he will ask me, 'if anyone has produced a fine speech or any other fine performance whatever, when you do not know the fine? And [b] when this is your condition, do you think you are better off alive than dead?'"

---

[9] 1972.
[10] 1977b. But cf. n. 19 below.
[11] Following Woodruff, 1982, and others I settle reluctantly on "fine" to English καλόν (admittedly lame, but the best we can do), asking the reader to bear constantly in mind that, quite unlike "fine," καλόν is the fundamental moral (as well as aesthetic) predicate in Greek discourse; the same is true, *mutatis mutandis*, of "foul" for αισχρόν.

At this last moment the comedy turns tragic. Socrates sees the failure of the definitional search as his personal disaster: if he has no viable answer to the question "What is the fine?" – and the long preceding discussion has shown that he hasn't – his life has lost its value, he might as well be dead.[12]

The first thing to notice here is something which passes completely unnoticed in published discussions of the "fallacy" prior to 1985:[13] all three of the texts I have cited come from post-elenctic dialogues, the *Lysis* and the *Hippias Major*, and have no clear precedent in any of the earlier dialogues.[14] In particular, there is no precedent for the alarmist view which proposition [G] leads Socrates to take of the failure of a search for the *F*. There is nothing remotely like this in preceding dialogues. There failure of a search for the *F* causes disappointment, not despair: Socrates gives no indication of regarding it as anything more than a temporary setback in an ongoing inquiry. In the *Euthyphro* he would have continued the search on the spot, were it not that the interlocutor, hurrying off, had dashed his hope to "learn from him" the nature of holiness.[15] In the *Laches* Socrates makes an appointment to return bright and early the next day to resume the search (201B–C). In the *Charmides* he blames, as usual, himself (175B5–6) for the failure of the search, but with no indication that he could do no better if he tried again. He finishes on an upbeat note, salvaging a large positive result, namely, that whatever temperance itself may turn out to be, it has already been shown to be a sufficient condition of happiness: Charmides is assured, "the more wise and temperate you are, the happier you will be" (176A).

The contrast with the state of mind depicted in T3 could hardly be

---

[12] Cf. n. 16 below.

[13] In Vlastos, 1985, I gave an abbreviated account of the dissolution of the "fallacy" on the terms I shall be expounding here. [The account was naturally omitted when GV revised the paper for chapter 2 of the present volume. – Ed.]

[14] I count as elenctic dialogues all and only those in which the elenchus, as defined in ch. I above, with Appendix, is Socrates' method of philosophical investigation. By that criterion the elenctic dialogues consist of *Ap., Ch., Cr., Eu., G., HMi., Ion, La., Pr., R.* 1 The quartet composed of *Ly., Eud., HMa.,* and *M.* is transitional to Plato's middle period, hence post-elenctic. No attention has been paid in the scholarly literature to the fact that T1, T2, and T3 all come from this latter group and cannot be presumed, in the absence of critical argument ad hoc, to voice views identical with those expressed in the former group, as is done e.g. by Santas, 1972: 134ff., Irwin, 1977: 40, Burnyeat, 1977b: 384 *et passim*, Woodruff, 1982: 138–9.

[15] 15E.

stronger. There Socrates sees catastrophe.[16] He says that if this is to be his condition – that of not knowing what is the fine and, therefore, not knowing if any particular action whatsoever is fine – he might as well be dead: his life is worthless. We know what would make life worthless for Socrates: forfeiture of virtue.[17] Thus Socrates is implying that since he cannot know if any particular action is fine so long as he has no definition of the "fine," he will be unable to tell if any action whatever, be it the noblest deed or the foulest crime, is fine or foul: all his practical moral judgments will be at sea; so he will be unable to make correct moral choices in his daily life and thus to act virtuously. He is morally bankrupt. Could Plato be telling us that this really happened to the Socrates of the elenctic dialogues – that this irrepressible gadfly, this mocking, taunting, aggressive, intrusive soul-saver, had believed a proposition that had crushed him? Surely that is the last thing Plato could be saying to us in those dialogues. There must be some way of blocking this impossible result.

The following, proposed and argued for by Irwin,[18] has also been accepted (independently) without argument by Burnyeat[19] and Santas,[20] and is also accepted by Woodruff.[21] Although Socrates cannot *know* if anything is F so long as he does not know what the F is, he may still have *true beliefs* about it and may use these to guide his life; true beliefs *sans* knowledge will suffice. Let me call this the "sufficiency of true belief" interpretation of the Socratic view ("*STB*" for short). Will this solve the problem? It might *if* it squared

---

[16] The gravity of the denouement at T3 has never been properly appreciated in the scholarly literature. Santas, who quotes and discusses T2, shows no awareness of the import of T3 (to which he makes no reference at all).

[17] *Cr.* 47D–48A; *G.* 512B1–2.

[18] 1977: 40–1.

[19] 1977b: 384ff. But the powerful polemical thrust of Burnyeat's paper has an altogether different target, demonstrating convincingly that Socrates does not treat examples as "little hard rocks of certainty" in the style of G. E. Moore (like "here is a hand" in Moore's famous refutation of idealism): Burnyeat shows that the test of the acceptability of Socratic examples is not brute common sense, but their ability to survive in a process of inquiry which is "typically an examination of the internal coherence of the views of Socrates' interlocutor" (384).

[20] 1979: 119ff. and 311, n. 26. (Here it appears as a belated afterthought to his previously expressed views on the "fallacy": no trace of it in his original response to Geach in 1972.)

[21] 1982: 140, who, however, seems to qualify his adherence to the view, substituting "tested opinion" for "belief."

with the textual evidence, as its sponsors have believed.[22] Well, does it? Let us recall some passages I cited in chapter 2:

T4 (= T9 in ch. 2), *G.* 505E4–5: "I think we should be contentiously eager *to know* what is true and what is false about the things we discuss."

T5 (= T10 in ch. 2), *G.* 472C6–D1: "For what we are debating are ... things which to know is noblest, *not to know* most base. For their sum and substance is to *know or not to know* who is happy and who is not."

What do the sponsors of *STB* propose to do with these texts? They do not say, apparently unaware that Socrates makes it clear in T4 that what he is after is knowledge, not just true belief; and in T5, that if he did not have knowledge, his condition would be "most base": no indication that his plight would be alleviated by true belief. Moreover he makes it clear that he has already reached the thing he is searching for – knowledge, not just true belief. Let me quote again a crucial text from chapter 2:

T6 (= T 12 in ch. 2) *G.* 486E5–6: "I *know* well that if you will agree with me on those things which my soul believes, those things will be the very truth."

On this text too there is no comment from the sponsors of *STB*. They seem content to ignore evidence that tells flatly against their claim that Socrates avows no more than true belief.

The clincher is T3 above. What Socrates' critic requires of him in part [a] is all too clearly moral *knowledge*: "How will you *know* ... when you do not *know* the fine?" Part [b] proceeds to spell out the dreadful consequence. On the *STB* interpretation, not knowing if any particular action is *F* would be innocuous, since one could still possess an ample stock of true beliefs. But in part [b] of T3 Socrates' critic tells him that *not knowing* if any particular action is *F* would spell moral disaster: no room is left here for getting by with true beliefs.

Clearly then *STB* will not do. It is inconsistent with texts which its sponsors accept as genuinely representative of the views of Socrates as expounded in Plato's earlier dialogues. We must look elsewhere for a solution. The hypothesis of the dual use of *to know* opens the way to it. Alerting us to those two possible uses of this verb, it

---

[22] Without ever confronting the strict implications of T3[b]: there is no discussion of these by any of the sponsors of *STB*.

prompts us to ask what Socrates would have made of proposition [G] in the elenctic dialogues if he had disambiguated "to know" in one or the other of those alternative ways. Suppose he had done so in the first way, understanding [G] to mean

[G_C]   If you do not know$_C$ what the F is, you will not know$_C$ if anything is F.

If so, G would have struck him as *vacuous*: having renounced knowledge$_C$ in the elenctic dialogues lock, stock, and barrel, he has no interest in knowing$_C$ if anything is F. If, however, it were disambiguated in the alternative way, taken to mean

[G_E]   If you do not know$_E$ what the F is, you will not know$_E$ if anything is F,

he would have seen it as *false*. If this is not clear right off, let me take time to make it clear.

If [G_E] were true, it would have a most embarrassing consequence: it would mean that if you do not already have a true elenctic definition of F it would be hopeless to try to reach it by one of Socrates' favorite methods of searching for definitions, namely, by investigating examples. For if [G_E] is true, then so long as you do not know what the F is, you will not know if any proposed examples are genuine; if they were bogus, they would be epistemically worthless: no inferences from them would have cognitive value. But when we scrutinize Socrates at work, we see him doing systematically what he would not be doing at all if he believed [G_E]: working towards the definition of the F from examples of it.[23] So, for example, in the *Laches*. Asked to say what courage is, Laches responds with an example:

T7 *La*. 190E: "By Zeus, Socrates, there is no difficulty in saying [what it is]. For if one is willing to stay in line to fight the enemy and does not run away, you know well that he is brave."

Laches is making a logical error. Asked for a definition, he gives an example as though the example were a definition. Socrates takes

---

[23] Santas in 1972 was the first to point this out, thereby taking the decisive step in the refutation of Geach's claim that Socrates thought [G] true.

pains to correct him. But in so doing he does not reject the example *qua* example. He agrees with it:

т8 *La.* 191A: "The man you speak of, who stays in the line and fights the enemy, he is brave, I suppose." Laches: "That is what I would say." Socrates: "I too."

To the example given him by Laches Socrates then proceeds to add a flock of his own:

т9 *La.* 191C–E: "For I wanted to ask you not only about those who are brave in the heavy infantry, but also about those in the cavalry and in every military formation; and also about those who are brave not only in perils of war but also in perils at sea, and those too who are brave in illness and in poverty and in politics; and, further, about those who are brave not only in pains and fears but are also tough in fighting desire or pleasure, firm in their ranks or turning against the enemy. There are people who are brave in these things too, Laches."

Flashing these motley cases before Laches, Socrates asks him to identify what it is to be brave by picking out their common feature. Could there be a more systematic violation of [G_E]? Nor is this all. To give Laches a model of the procedure that should be followed Socrates shows him how a definition of "quickness" might be reached. He puts up a slew of examples (quick running, quick strumming, quick talking, quick learning), hits on a neat little formula that captures what all these have in common ("doing much in little time"), holds up the formula as a paradigm and asks Laches to do the same in the case of courage. Is it not clear that in the *Laches* [G_E] is as far as anything could be from what Socrates believes?

But are those examples genuine? Does Socrates know$_E$ that the ones he listed are bona fide cases of courage? He puts them forward in elenctic argument as his personal beliefs, confident that he can defend them *more elenctico*; and they pass unchallenged. This suffices for presumptive knowledge$_E$.[24] Only if they were successfully attacked by elenctic argument would they be unsettled. As for the examples of quickness, he would not be making them the base of a model definition, unless he did know$_E$ that they were unimpeachable, as they trivially are in plain common sense.

---

[24] See additional note 3.1, "Presumptive moral knowledge."

So once we apply the know$_C$/know$_E$ ambiguity, proposition [G] turns out to be a paper tiger. If Socrates read it as [G$_C$] he would have thumbed his nose at it, for it would then be irrelevant to his search for moral knowledge: it may be true for all he knows or cares, but its truth would have no bearing on his quest, since knowledge$_C$ is none of his concern. If he had read it as [G$_E$], on the other hand, he would reckon it patently false, posing no threat to his search for knowledge$_E$ of the F by means of examples.

How is it then that [G] ever came to be pinned on him in the scholarly literature? The answer is that texts which prompted the imputation had been misread. Here is the most important of them, probably the very one which suggested [G] to Geach in his reading of the *Euthyphro*:[25]

T10 *Eu.* 6E3–6: "Explain this character (*idean*) to me – what on earth is it? – so that by looking to it and using it as a standard (*paradeigma*) I shall say of whatever you or anyone else may do of that sort that it is holy, and if it is not of that sort I shall say that it is not."

Is Socrates really implying here that he accepts proposition [G]? So Geach and others have thought – but only because they read the text with deplorable looseness.[26] What [G] stipulates is that knowing what the F is constitutes a *necessary* condition of knowing if anything is F. What T10 stipulates is that knowing what the F is constitutes a *sufficient* condition of knowing if anything is F. Stated formally, for comparison with [G], the import of T10 is

[G*]   If you do know what the F is, you will know if you are predicating "F" correctly about anything whatever – you will know if anything is F.

Only if we were to confuse a sufficient with a necessary condition would we take Socrates' acceptance of [G*] as evidence of his acceptance of [G] in an elenctic dialogue.

If we did not make this mistake it would not occur to us to impute to the Socrates of this and other elenctic dialogues the catastrophic

---

[25] I say "probably" because Geach does not refer to T10 as such. There are precious few references to texts in his paper, leaving us to guess what it was that led him to charge Socrates so confidently with the "Socratic fallacy."

[26] As Santas was the first to point out (1972: 136).

consequences of [G]. There is nothing in [G*] that Socrates would have found the least bit disturbing. In [G*] he voices the belief that if he were to find the thing he is looking for he would come into possession of a wonderful thing: a criterion for settling all those vexing disputes over controversial cases, like the one that sets the stage for Socrates' encounter with Euthyphro. A hired man on the paternal estate in Naxos kills, in a drunken fit, one of the slaves. The father ties up the killer hand and foot, lowers him into a ditch, and sends a messenger to the exegetes, asking for advice on what he ought to do; by the time the word comes back the hired man has died from hypothermia, dehydration, and lack of food. The father is clearly responsible for the man's death. Is Euthyphro acting piously in prosecuting his own father for killing a hired man who is himself a killer?[27] Euthyphro says that he "knows [this] exactly (ἀκριβῶς)" (5A1-2).[28] But it is indignantly rejected by the father and all his kin: the family consider it downright impious of Euthyphro to initiate prosecution which, if successful, would have terrible consequences[29] for his own father.[30] What Socrates is saying in [G*] is that if one did have the definition of "piety," one would be able to resolve this nasty dispute: one would know clearly[31] if Euthyphro's prosecution of his father is or is not pious.

This is as far as Socrates ever moves in the direction of [G] in an elenctic dialogue. Let us reflect on how far this still leaves him from it. Acceptance of [G] would have been paralyzing for a search like the one in the *Laches*: if he had conceded [G] he would have lost his start in that search, for according to [G] there is *no* case he could count as bona fide courage without prior knowledge of its definition. His search would have been doomed to failure before it started. Not

---

[27] Under Athenian law there is no prosecution of homicide except by members of the victim's kin.

[28] Cf. n. 31 below.

[29] Exile or death.

[30] Contemporary sentiment reckons injuries to parents as cases of impiety no less than offenses to the gods. In Andocides (*Myst.* 19) it is taken for granted that it would be ἀνοσιώτατον to give damaging information about one's own father.

[31] As Euthyphro had claimed he did: asked if he did have "exact" knowledge of divine things which enabled him to know that he was acting piously in prosecuting his father (4E4-8), he had assured Socrates that he did (4E9-5A2). At the close of the dialogue, when it has become all too clear that Euthyphro's claim to have such knowledge was bogus, Socrates reminds him mockingly of it and challenges him to make it good (15D4-E1).

so if all he accepted were [G*]: nothing in this to tell him that if he doesn't already have the answer to "What is the *F*?" he can't count on any of those ordinary, utterly uncontroversial cases, as examples of the *F* from which he could reason to new ones by analogy. Only if he had believed in the truth of [G], as he does in the *Lysis* and the *Hippias Major*, would he have found himself in that predicament.

At this juncture I must point out that a parallel difference between elenctic and post-elenctic dialogues obtains in the case of what Richard Robinson had termed "the priority of definition." This is the logical twin of [G], which I shall call "proposition [R]"[32] in his honour:[33]

[R]   If you do not know what the *F* is, you will not know if you are predicating correctly anything about the *F* – you will not know anything about the *F*.

As Robinson noted, this proposition plays a great role in the *Meno*. The dialogue begins with it. Asked if virtue is teachable, Socrates replies (I omit the preliminary palaver):

T11 *M*. 71A–B: "I am so far from knowing whether or not it is teachable, that I do not even know in the least what virtue itself is ... Of that which I do not know what it is (τί ἐστιν), how could I know of what sort it is (ὁποῖόν τι [ἐστιν])?"

Going through the motions of pursuing the original question in the first third of the dialogue, Socrates does not waive his initial objection. He reinstates it when the search gets stuck at 80A–B and Meno brings up the "eristic paradox" to crow over the mishap (80D5–8). Socrates does not reject the paradox. He uses it (80E1–5) *in propria persona* to show the disastrous consequence of [R]. Let me fill out his reasoning:

If you don't have prior knowledge of what virtue is, you will not know anything about virtue.

---

[32] Cf. n. 6 above.
[33] Since he did more than anyone else to bring it under scrutiny. It is under his influence that Ross comes upon it (1951: 12, n. 4), and he does nothing to advance its discussion beyond the point where Robinson had left it.

If you don't know anything about it, you will not know what you
   are looking for.
If you don't know what you are looking for, it is futile to search for
   it. Ergo, if you don't have prior knowledge of what virtue is, it
   is futile to search for it.

Socrates does not try to break through this impasse. He breaks
away from it by the wildest flight on which Plato's metaphysical
imagination ever took off, the theory of "recollection": he has learned
from priests and priestesses that the soul has a prenatal history
reaching far into the primordial past where it once had learned
everything[34] and henceforth carries this marvellous cargo of omni-
science deep in its unconscious, whence pieces of it can be dredged
up to yield what Plato has come to regard as real knowledge – not
knowledge$_E$, but knowledge$_C$. To explore the import of this new
doctrine would take us into the darkest strata of Plato's thought. All
that is profound and obscure in his epistemology and metaphysics
is rooted there. Since I must stay close to the topic of the present
essay, all I need remark about his new doctrine is that it is about
as far as it could be from anything we could associate with the
Socrates of the elenctic dialogues. This, if anything, is what Socrates
would have called "more than human knowledge"[35] in the elenctic
dialogues. If it had crossed his mind at all he would have left it
for the gods and for those of his fellow-mortals whose folly, venal
or sublime, beguiles them into violating the pious precept that
"mortals must think mortal."[36] When Plato puts this new doctrine
into the mouth of Socrates we know that the protagonist of the
elenctic dialogues has achieved euthanasia in a genius greater than
his own – Plato's.

When Socrates is made to embrace this new doctrine in the *Meno*,
he is not allowed to forget proposition [R]. He recalls it twice. He
does so first when he resumes, with the aid of the method of

---

[34] "The soul being immortal and having had many births and seen both the things in this
world and those in Hades and everything, there is nothing it has not come to know" (81c).

[35] *Ap.* 20D6–E2, quoted as T31 in chapter 2.

[36] θνητὰ φρονεῖν: Euripides, *Ba.* 395–7; Sophocles, *Trach.* 473; Aristotle, *N.E.* 1177b31–4,
(quoted as T33–T35 in chapter 2).

"hypothesis," borrowed from the mathematicians,[37] the inquiry into whether virtue is or is not teachable. Just before reopening the search on these new terms Socrates warns Meno:

T12 *M*. 86D–E: "If I had you, no less than myself, under control, we would not investigate whether or not virtue is teachable, before inquiring first what it is."

Then, at the dialogue's very end, Socrates reiterates the objection to searching for the answer to some question about the *F* without prior knowledge of what the *F* itself is. The dialogue closes on that note:

T13 *M*. 100B: "Clear knowledge of [this][38] we shall reach [only] when we shall undertake to inquire what virtue is itself by itself, before [inquiring] how it comes to be present in men."

So in this post-elenctic dialogue, later than the *Lysis* and the *Hippias Major*,[39] commitment to proposition [R] is as clear as is the commitment to proposition [G] in these. But if it had occurred to Socrates earlier on in the elenctic dialogues, it would have had no terrors for him. He would only have needed to apply to it the same disambiguation that disarms [G]. If "know" in [R] is read as "know$_C$," the proposition becomes

[R$_C$] If you don't know$_C$ what the *F* is, you will not know$_C$ anything about the *F*.

In the elenctic dialogues, [R$_C$] would not have caused Socrates to turn a hair: at that time, having no interest in knowing$_C$ anything at all, he has no interest in knowing$_C$ anything about the *F*. Alternatively, if he had read its "know" as "know$_E$," it would turn into [R$_E$],

[R$_E$] If you don't know$_E$ what the *F* is, you will not know$_E$ anything about the *F*,

---

[37] ἐξ ὑποθέσεως σκοπεῖσθαι, 86E. This method enables Socrates to search for the *F* without violation of [R]: hypothesizing that the *F* is *K* and that *K* is *L* he reaches the *hypothetical* result that the *F* is *L*, which will not constitute knowledge$_C$ of the *F* until it has been "bound by reasoning out the *aitia*" (*M*. 98A), i.e. integrated in systematized knowledge predicated on the definition of the *F*.

[38] Sc. on whether virtue may come by "divine dispensation" in those who do not have knowledge.

[39] Since it contains, as they do not, the doctrine of the transmigrating, "recollecting" soul which characterizes the middle dialogues.

and this would have struck him as patently false. Thus the Socrates of the *Gorgias* has plenty of knowledge$_E$ about justice – for example, he knows$_E$[40] that those who stick by it regardless of cost to any and all of their other interests, are always happier than those who don't. Yet he had not assayed any definition of "justice" and there is no indication that, if he had tried, he would have been able to produce an elenctically viable answer to the "What is *F*?" question for *F* = "justice." And so it would be throughout the elenctic dialogues. Socrates' knowledge$_E$ about the *F* whose definition he does not manage to discover is what guides him through his searches for it and enables him to make very substantial progress in insight into the *F* in spite of failing to reach the answer to "What is the *F*?" which is the formal end of those inquiries. Thus in the *Euthyphro* Socrates establishes by elenctic argument, hence knows$_E$, that the nature of holiness does not depend on whether or not the gods happen to like it, but that their liking it is determined by its own nature. This proposition, which may be hailed as the foundation of a rational religion, is established securely at *Euthyphro* 11A, and stands untouched by the *aporia* which besets Socrates later on, when the dialogue winds up without having discovered the answer to the question "What is holiness?" The same would be true in the case of the *F* searched for in the *Laches*, the *Charmides*, and *Republic* 1.[41] In none of the elenctic dialogues does the unavailability of knowledge$_E$ of the definition of the *F* keep Socrates from knowing$_E$ a great deal about it and using that partial knowledge$_E$ to search for the knowledge of the nature of the *F* which still eludes him.

What reason then could there be for imputing to him acceptance of [R] in those dialogues? None. It was only because of the unwarranted assumption that what Socrates believes in a transitional

---

[40] I.e. is in a position to show that the thesis that to commit injustice is worse than to suffer it is elenctically viable: *G.* 509A, "of all those I have encountered no one has been able to hold otherwise and fail to come off covered with ridicule [in elenctic argument]."

[41] It remains true all through *R.* 1 until 354 A11, which I take to be the whole of the original dialogue to which 354A12–C3 is tacked on as a graceful bridge to *R.* 11 when Plato makes this dialogue the prelude to *R.* 11–x: cf. Vlastos, 1985: n. 65, and *Socrates*, additional note 2.1. "The composition of *Republic* 1." That this closing paragraph could not have belonged to the original dialogue is shown by the contradiction between Socrates' saying at 354C1–2 that, since he does not know what justice is, he cannot know whether or not it is a virtue, and his earlier claim to have shown that no one could fail to know (hence Socrates could not) that justice is a virtue (351A3–6).

dialogue like the *Meno* he must also have believed in the elenctic
dialogues which precede it that he was saddled with the acceptance
of [R] in these. When Robinson cites [R], documenting it, correctly
enough, extensively from the *Meno*,[42] he adds a reference to the
Protagoras,[43] without the least suspicion that what is all too true in a
late transitional dialogue might not hold true at all in an earlier one,
like the *Protagoras*. Here is the text to which he refers:

> T14 *Pr.* 360E6–361A3: "I ask all those questions only because I want to
> investigate how matters stand with regard to virtue[44] and what on earth virtue
> itself is.[45] For I know that when this has been brought to light the thing on
> which you and I have, each of us, spun out such long arguments, will become
> perfectly clear (κατάδηλον) – I maintaining that virtue is not teachable, you
> maintaining that it is."

Is Socrates evidencing here acceptance of proposition [R]? So it
looks superficially. But let us look again. What he is saying in T14 is
that if he did find the thing he is looking for – the answer to "what
virtue itself is" – then the answer to the question he and Protagoras
have been debating, "Is virtue teachable?", would "become perfectly clear", i.e. that knowing what the *F* is would disclose knowledge of whether or not it is teachable – would be a *sufficient* condition
for knowing this particular thing about it. This is altogether different from claiming that knowing what the *F* is is a *necessary* condition for knowing *anything whatever* about it. Once alerted to that
difference we can see that in taking T14 as evidence of [R] Robinson
made the same mistake that Geach must have made in taking T10
above as evidence of [G]. Once the mistake is corrected we can see
that the true import of T14 when it is correctly read is not [R], but

[R*]   If you do know what the *F* is, you will know whether or not
you are predicating correctly anything about the *F* – you will know
whether or not the *F* is anything –

for example, in the case of *F* = "virtue," you will know whether or
not virtue is teachable. So too in what he proceeds to state when he

---

[42] His first three references (1953: 50) are to T11, T12, T13.
[43] And he is not the only one: T14 is regularly cited in the scholarly literature as evidence of
the presence of the "Socratic fallacy" in the form of [R] in elenctic dialogues.
[44] πῶς ποτ' ἔχει τὰ περὶ ἀρετῆς.
[45] τί ποτ' ἔστιν αὐτό, ἡ ἀρετή.

reiterates, a few lines later, the point made in T14:

T15 *Pr.* 361c2–6: "Seeing these things in utter confusion I have the greatest desire to clear them up and would wish that having got through them we should come to the question of what virtue is. Then we could return to figure out if virtue is or is not teachable."

When the answer to the question "What is virtue?" has been reached – and no doubt of the possibility of reaching it is voiced either here or previously in T14 – *then* we would have the ground on which we could answer the question "Is it teachable?"

If Robinson had distinguished [R] from [R*] he would have realized that proposition [R] has entered the Platonic corpus no earlier than the *Meno*, and that what we find in lieu of it in the earliest dialogues is a proposition easily mistakable for it that has radically different import for Socrates' elenctic searches. The import of [R] for these would have been paralyzingly defeatist: [R] would have told him that it is folly to embark on searches for knowledge about the *F* if he does not already have an answer to "What is the *F*?" [R*], on the other hand, instead of discouraging Socrates from embarking on those searches, would offer him a powerful lure for pursuing them, holding out the promise of a wonderful illumination if they were to succeed, *without saying anything whatever to imply that they could not succeed.* [R*] tells him that the things he wants to know about courage, temperance, justice, piety, virtue would become clear to him if he could but reach that longed-for result. And since there is nothing but his own sloth to keep him from trying, try he would, as we see him doing in the elenctic dialogues regardless of setbacks, for nothing is said or implied in [R*] to dampen his hopes of reaching that objective if he keeps trying again and again.

But why should it be, it may be asked, that [R] (and, for that matter, [G] too) should have remained sleepers in Plato's elenctic dialogues, waking up to plague Socrates only in the transitionals? Why did the alarm-clock go off then, and not before? Readers of my essay, "Elenchus and mathematics,"[46] would know my answer to this question. The grand hypothesis I defend there collects the evidence that it is only in transitional dialogues that knowledge of

---

[46] Vlastos, 1988 (*Socrates*, ch. 4).

advanced mathematics becomes a vital force in Plato's thought, and it is *there* that [G] and [R] show up, as they never did before. So long as your inquiries concern exclusively moral questions, as they do for Socrates throughout the elenctic dialogues, it makes perfect sense to say that you do know examples of the *F* without having come to know what the *F* is (i.e. that [G] is false) and that you similarly know many propositions about the *F*, while still lacking a definition of the *F* (i.e. that [R] is false). For moral terms hail from common speech, where their meaning is established long before you could undertake to encapsulate it in a Socratic definition. Not so if the terms you are investigating are going to range over geometrical entities – squares, circles, lines, points and the like. The method now established so firmly in geometry that only cranks feel free to deviate from it requires you to put into your axiom-set, *in advance of the proof of any theorem*, definitions of every *F* whose properties are determinable by geometrical reasoning. In geometry, whose domain is that of knowledge$_C$, not knowledge$_E$, propositions [G] and [R] *must* be read as [G$_C$] and [R$_C$], and then they will be true, non-vacuously so.

Just think of the truth discovered in the interrogation of the slave-boy in the *Meno*. If what you are after is geometrical proof, the crucial lemma at 84E4–85A1, that the diagonal bisects its square[47] (whose intuitive grasp suffices for heuristic purposes in leading the boy to the discovery of the theorem), would be useless *unless* your terms had been correctly defined, beginning with "square," where you might think a definition is superfluous, since, after all, "square" is a term in common speech: everyone uses it all the time, so no one needs a definition to know what it means. But look at what happens in the interrogation of the boy. There (82B9–C3) "square" is identified by pointing to the figure in the sand and telling the boy that a square is a figure "like this," "with four equal sides," i.e. as an equilateral (rectilinear quadrilateral). But, as everyone would know who had even the rudiments of geometry, to fix only in this way the meaning of "square" would be to court disaster. For this would not

---

[47] "Now does this line from corner to corner cut each of these figures [squares] in half?"

distinguish the figure from a rhombus, which is also an equilateral (rectilinear quadrilateral), but has other properties radically differ- ent from a square's. So if you had not made sure that what you are talking about is uniquely and exclusively a square, everything could go wrong after that: if the bisected figure had been a rhombus the lemma would still be true, but the theorem would not follow from the lemma; the square on the diagonal of a rhombus does *not* dupli- cate its area. So in geometry what Geach had stigmatized as a "fallacy" would be no fallacy, but the plain truth: to know that you are predicating "square" of anything in a demonstration you would have to know the definition of that term. So [G] would be true. And so would [R]: knowing the definition of "square" would be a neces- sary condition of knowing that the square on a square's diagonal duplicates its area.

On the hypothesis I defended in 1988 and now again in the present chapter it was Plato, under the spell of his own deepening mathematical interests, who realized how crucial was definition for success in the search for knowledge$_{\rm c}$, and therefore moved [R$_{\rm C}$] into the center of his representation of the Socratic profession of ignorance when he came to write the *Meno*. Thus had it not been for Plato's mathematical studies which had become so absorbing as to dominate the exposition of the two great novelties of the *Meno* – the doctrine of "recollection" and "investigating by hypothesis" – we would have heard nothing of the "Socratic fallacy." We hear noth- ing of it even as late as the *Gorgias*, where Socrates' disclaimer of knowledge$_{\rm C}$ is still as forceful as ever yet so vague in content as to express no more than the conviction that the elenctic method was powerless to yield the iron-clad certainty traditionally expected of all knowledge worthy of the name. Ascription to him of the "Socratic fallacy" is a retrojection of a feature of transitional dialogues, the *Lysis*, *Hippias Major*, and *Meno*, upon dialogues which precede them – an accident of Geach's and Robinson's failure to perceive the radical difference in outlook between the period in which Plato was advancing in mathematical studies, and that of his earlier period, when he was still a faithful Socratic, and his "Socrates" was the moralist, pure and simple, who knew nothing and cared nothing about current developments in mathematical science,[48] all of his energies absorbed in investigating exclusively moral topics and practicing faithfully the elenctic method. From the "fallacy", of which Socrates has been convicted by a loose reading of Platonic texts,[49] more exact reading of those same texts acquits him.

---

[48] The exploration of irrationals and the development of the axiomatic method. We have evidence that Plato had caught up with the first when he wrote the *Hippias Major* (303B–C: cf. *Socrates*, ch. 4, 126–7) and with the second when he wrote the *Meno* (76A: cf. *Socrates*, ch. 4, 120–2).

[49] Principally of T10 and T14 above, but of much else as well that might have alerted scholars to the large differences between elenctic and post-elenctic dialogues.

4

THE HISTORICAL SOCRATES
AND ATHENIAN DEMOCRACY[1]

I shall argue for two principal theses:

I. In his own time and place Socrates was widely perceived as
μισόδημος, i.e. as anti-populist (literally, as "people-hater"[2]).
II. This public perception of him was a misperception: he had not
been the crypto-oligarch many had thought he was.

On Thesis I I shall not linger long. The evidence for it can be
quickly laid out, beginning with

T1 Aeschines, *Against Timarchus* 173: "Men of Athens, you executed Socrates
the sophist because he was shown to have educated Critias, one of the Thirty
who put down the democracy."[3]

This shows that half a century after Socrates' death a lot-selected
jury – a fair sample of Athenian public opinion at the time – was
expected to agree without argument that Socrates had been put to
death because he had been the teacher of the man who stood in
living memory as the leader of the most savagely anti-democratic

---

[1] An earlier version of this essay was delivered on 14 February 1983, at the University of
London as an S. V. Keeling Lecture and elicited helpful criticism from colleagues who heard
it there. The present version is a revision of the text of an address presented six weeks later
at a conference on Ancient Greek Political Theory at the Graduate Center of the City
University of New York, organized by Professor Melvin Richter, and published in *Political
Theory* II (1983), 495–516.

[2] See n. 3 below.

[3] τὸν δῆμον καταλυσάντων. In fourth-century Attic prose, δῆμος often continues to do double
duty, standing "for both the ruling power in a democracy and for the constitutional form of
its rule" (Vlastos, *Platonic Studies* [hereafter "*PS*"], 167: many references to the literature
there), as it had done originally in fifth-century prose, before the creation of the term
δημοκρατία (as in the debate on constitutions in Herodotus 3.81.3 *et passim*). It is so used in
μισόδημος, expressing both upper-class contemptuous hostility for the common people and
hostile disapproval of democracy itself.

regime Athens had ever known. The lapse of time which separates it from the event of which it speaks does not erode its evidential value. Aeschines had heard much about those years from his own father, Atrometus. He had gone into exile under the Thirty to join the embattled democrats under Thrasybulus who restored the democracy; "the misfortunes of the city [at that time] were a household word with us, dinned into my ears."[4]

And now consider how a powerful politician's relation to a "sophist" who had once been his teacher was popularly regarded at the time:

T2 Plutarch, *Pericles* 4.1:   Most people say that [Pericles'] teacher of music was Damon ... Now Damon seems to have been a consummate sophist. He had used music as a screen to hide his cleverness from the public. In his relation to Pericles he was in politics what a coach and trainer is to an athlete. (Cf. also Aristotle, *Ath. Pol.* 27.4)[5]

What to us seems so preposterous – that a brilliant statesman's role in public affairs could be accounted for by the personal effect of a sophist's teaching – was evidently not thought at all implausible at, or near, Socrates' own lifetime: the fourth-century historians on whom Plutarch is drawing in T2, Aristotle among them, find no difficulty in believing that the radical reforms by which Pericles changed the course of Athenian history had been put into his head by a sophist who had taught him music.[6] Aeschines and his Athenian audience would have found no greater difficulty in believing that Critias' sensational political career had been instigated by a sophist who had taught him rhetoric. We thus have evidence from an unimpeachable source – an orator untinctured by philosophy, caring nothing one way or the other about it, and having no partisan axe to grind by representing Socrates as a pro-oligarchic ideologue – that Socrates, because of his association with Critias, was believed half a century after his death to have been a breeder of subversion.

It is a reasonable inference that the same would be true at the

---

[4] Aeschines, *On the Embassy* 78.
[5] For the use of these two texts to illuminate T1 I am indebted to Dover, 1976.
[6] Pericles' most radical innovation – pay for dicastic service – is specifically ascribed by Aristotle to Damon's "advice."

time of Socrates' trial, when Critias' crimes were so much more fresh in everyone's mind: no less sinister a construction would be likely to be put on that association and, we may add, also on his association with Alcibiades, a notorious contemner of democracy (Thuc. 6.89.5).

T3 Xenophon, *Mem.* 1.2.12: "But the accuser said that Critias and Alcibiades, having associated with Socrates, did great evil to the city."

For this inference we have excellent confirmation:

T4 Xenophon, *Mem.* 1.2.9: "But, by Zeus, said the accuser, he made his associates despise the established laws, saying it was silly to appoint the city's magistrates by lot, when no one would want to use a lot-selected pilot or builder or flute-player or any other [craftsman] for work in which mistakes are far less disastrous than those which concern the city."

In marked contrast to every other charge against Socrates rehearsed in the *Memorabilia*, to all of which Xenophon responds with voluble apologetics, this charge Xenophon must think so true and so firmly entrenched in his readers' minds that he does not say a word to rebut it: he drops it like a hot potato.

So unless there were direct evidence to the contrary, the first part of my first thesis would stand: Socrates was perceived as a politically subversive teacher, and this perception of him would have certainly weighed strongly in the motives of the prosecution and in the minds of many of the jurors who had voted for his conviction. And there is no evidence to the contrary. As has long been recognized, the fact that the imputation of subversion does not surface in the formal indictment does not constitute such evidence, for this fact is perfectly explicable by the amnesty: to substantiate the imputation in court Socrates' tutorial link to Critias or other leaders of the oligarchic coup would have had to be rehearsed, and this would have been a violation of the amnesty. Thus Socrates could only have been formally indicted on charges which either were not political at all – not believing in the gods of the state and introducing new divinities – or only indirectly political: corrupting the youth.[7] That these charges were not just window-dressing – the mere "pretexts" Burnet called

---

[7] For political implications in this charge see *Cr.* 53B7–C3, noting the connection of "corruptor of the laws" at B7 with "corruptor of young and unintelligent men" at C2.

them (1914:189) – is abundantly clear from the Platonic *Apology* (22E–23E): Socrates had provoked powerful enmities by blasting the credibility of big mouths in Athens and they, retaliating, had done their best to get people to believe that the Aristophanic caricature, a comic extravaganza, had been in fact the ugly truth. We thus have evidence that Socrates was prosecuted and convicted *both* as impious speculator and shyster rhetorician, on the one hand, *and* as a fomenter of oligarchic sentiment, on the other. Scholars like R. Hackforth (1933: 73ff.), who adduced evidence of the former as though it constituted evidence against the latter, were simply confused: there is no inconsistency between the two, since in the public image of Socrates the pestilential sophist *was* the subversive.

Now to my second thesis. I maintain that the perception of Socrates as a pro-oligarchic ideologist who aroused hostility towards the Athenian constitution in his associates was completely false: false it must have been if Socrates preferred that constitution to every other in the contemporary world – which is precisely what we are told in one of the most familiar, yet least heeded, passages in the Platonic corpus: *Crito* 51C4–53C8. Of all the commentators consulted, only one – George Grote, in his monumental 1865: vol. I, 302–4 – has discerned what I take to be the true import of this passage: that it is "a piece of rhetoric imbued with the most genuine spirit of constitutional democracy"; that here "Socrates is made to express the feelings and repeat the language of a devoted democratical patriot." Grote must have thought that this would be so evident to anyone who would but read the passage that he offered no argument at all for this interpretation of the text. Since the passage has been read very differently by other scholars I must supply the argument, even at the risk of laboring the obvious.

Socrates is explaining why he must decline the opportunity Crito has offered him to escape. His explanation is put into a discourse by the personified laws of Athens. Since the latter are Socrates' mouthpiece – what they say is what he makes them say – the sentiments they impute to him must be his own.[8] I shall, therefore, report them

---

[8] Attempts to drive a wedge between the discourse of the Laws and Socrates' own opinions are repeatedly made. I have yet to see evidence for them which stands up to examination. Thus, most recently, Woodruff, 1983:94, claims that the discourse "appeals to the false view

as such. The sentiment on which they dwell at greatest length is his affection for Athens and its laws – a sentiment that has the intensity of a romantic attachment:

T5 *Cr.* 52B1–C1: "O Socrates, we have strong proof that both we and the city have been pleasing to you. For you would not have been, above other Athenians, exceedingly constant in your residence in the city, if it were not exceedingly pleasing to you. Not even for a festival did you ever go out of Athens, except once to the Isthmian games – nowhere else, except on military service; nor did you make any out-of-town visits, like other folk, nor did the desire ever seize you to know some other city, some other laws: you have been satisfied with us and with our city."

Like an infatuated lover, Socrates can hardly bring himself to part a single day from his beloved Athens. What is it that keeps him so glued to it over the years? The only thing he mentions here is Athens' laws. The city and its laws appear conjunctively at the start ("both we and the city have been pleasing to you") and then again at the conclusion ("you have been satisfied with us and with our city"). The conjunction is maintained in the sequel:

T6 *Cr.* 52C1–3: "So intensely did you prefer us (οὕτω σφόδρα ἡμᾶς ᾑροῦ) and agree to conduct your civic life in accordance with us that, among other things, you had children in it (sc. the city), which shows that the city pleased you (ὡς ἀρεσκούσης σοι τῆς πόλεως)."

I translate ᾑροῦ (literally "chose") in οὕτω σφόδρα ἡμᾶς ᾑροῦ by "preferred": that this is what is meant is clear both from the context (the choice in favor of the laws of Athens [ἡμᾶς ᾑροῦ] is depicted throughout the passage[9] as expressing a *preference* for its laws over those of other cities) and from the qualifying adverb (not choice *per se*, but preference, could be properly spoken of as "intense"). So the same decision – to raise a family in Athens – is viewed first as evidencing a preference for the city's *laws* ("so intensely did you prefer *us*") and then again, without any interjected explanation, as

that how people react to Socrates is morally relevant" (but the allusion at 54B7 is not to "people" but "to your own people" – people for whose opinion you do care) and "appears to presuppose the odious possibility that in cases not involving parents and guardians it could be permissible to return harm for harm" (but what is permissible at 50E6 is ἀντιποιεῖν, *not* ἀνταδικεῖν and ἀντικακουργεῖν, which are clearly ruled out at 54C2–3).
[9] Explicitly so at 52E5–53A5: "But you did not prefer either Sparta or Crete, which you are always saying are well-governed, nor any other city, Greek or barbarian ... So clear it is that to you, above other Athenians, the city and we the laws are exceedingly pleasing: for whom would a city please without the laws?"

evidencing his preference for the *city* ("which shows that the *city* pleased you."). The very structure of the sentence shows that the object of Socrates' preference is the same in each case: what pleases Socrates in the city is its laws; the laws speak of the city as "our city" (T5 above) and proceed to ask: "whom would a city please without the laws?"[10]

Now what is it in the laws of Athens that Socrates prefers to the laws of "every other city, Greek or barbarian," including the laws of Sparta and Crete[11] and of Thebes and Megara?[12] What is it that sets off Athens most dramatically from all four of those "well-governed"[13] cities? In respect of its civil and criminal law Athens would differ little from its neighbors – scarcely at all from Megara, a highly commercial city, whose economy, and hence its civil law, would be in all essentials identical with that of Athens. The salient difference – the one that would leap to the eye of any Greek juxtaposing Athens against that quartet of cities – would be in the area of constitutional law.[14] In the Athenian constitution democracy reached its apogee in fifth-century Greece, while each of those four constitutions stood as clearly for oligarchy – extreme in the case of the Spartan and Cretan constitutions, moderate in the case of the Theban and Megarian. So while no mention is made of either democracy or oligarchy anywhere in the passage, there can be no doubt that Socrates' preference for Athenian law is *a preference for Athens' democratic constitution*. Each of the four oligarchies Socrates hails as "well-governed" – as well he might in the case of Sparta and Crete, exemplars of law-governed, law-respecting, law-observing conduct throughout the Greek world (cf. Hdt. 7.104). If Socrates

[10] N. 9 above *sub fin.*

[11] N. 9 above.

[12] *Cr.* 53B.

[13] That εὐνομεῖσθαι as applied to Sparta and Crete at 52E and to Thebes and Megara at 53B refers primarily to good observance of the laws (rather than to the possession of good laws as such) is clear in the latter passage: that Thebes and Megara εὐνομοῦνται is given as the explanation of the hostile reception Socrates would get in those cities if he arrived there as jail-breaker and "corruptor of the laws."

[14] In the converse case, when Socrates is accused of fomenting disrespect for the "laws" of Athens, its constitution is clearly what is meant. The passage in Xenophon quoted in T4 above continues: "Such arguments, said he [the accuser], led the young to despise the established *constitution* [a variant expression for 'the established laws' at the start of the quotation] and made them violent."

were comparing Athens on this score with Sparta and Crete or even with Thebes and Megara, he would certainly prefer any of them to Athens for, as we shall see, he thinks the Athenian record of law-observance deplorably low. Thus his preference for Athenian over Spartan, Cretan, Theban and Megarian law could only be a preference for the democratic form of government over the leading specimens of oligarchy. He ranks the ultrademocratic constitution of the undisciplined Athenians above the oligarchic constitution of the disciplined ("well-governed") Thebans and Megarians and the still more undemocratic constitution of the still more disciplined Spartans and Cretans.

Can we take him at his word? If so, the case for my second thesis has been made. Is there any reason why we can't? To deny or doubt Socrates' preference for the Athenian constitution which is expressed so forcefully in the *Crito* we would have to be convinced of one or the other or both of the following:

(1) That this preference is contradicted by other sentiments expressed by Socrates elsewhere in Plato's Socratic dialogues,[15]

(2) That it is contradicted by opinions voiced by Socrates in Xenophon, our other major source, and that we have evidence independent of both Xenophon and Plato for rating Xenophon's credibility on this point more highly than Plato's.

I shall argue that Plato's testimony in the *Crito* passage, as interpreted above, is unassailable on either of these grounds and should, therefore, be accepted as true.

On the first of those two points I can be fairly brief. No harsher indictment of Athenian public conduct has survived than the one Plato puts into Socrates' mouth in the *Apology*:

T7 *Ap.* 31D–E: "Fellow Athenians, you should know that, if I had tried to do politics (πράττειν τὰ πολιτικά) long before this, I would have perished long before this, without doing any good either to you or to myself. Don't be incensed at me for telling you the truth. There isn't a man who would survive if

---

[15] Throughout this chapter I proceed on the hypothesis (for which I argue elsewhere) that in this early part of his corpus (and *only* here) Plato re-creates views and arguments of the historical Socrates, depicting them in conversations which are, for the most part, dramatic fiction rather than biography. For the dialogues which, in my view, fall into this part of the Platonic corpus see additional note 1.1.

he really set himself to oppose you or any other multitude, trying to block the perpetration of many injustices and illegalities in the city."

He is telling his fellow-citizens that their political life is such a jungle of lawlessness and injustice that a just man who gets into it determined to fight for justice is virtually signing his own death warrant. In the *Gorgias* there is a no less savage attack on democratic leadership. Its theme is that in Athenian politics the ticket to power is flattery of the *demos*. This is the first thing Socrates tells Callicles at the start of their debate, barely managing to avoid the extreme rudeness, the gross insult, of the imputation by resorting to banter, ringing the changes on an atrocious pun: Callicles is as ingratiating to the Athenian *demos* as to his young inamorato whose name is "Demos".

T8 *G.* 481D1–E3: "It strikes me that you and I have had the same experience – each of us has two loves: in my case, Alcibiades, son of Cleinias, and philosophy; in yours, the Athenian *demos* and Pyrilampes' son, Demos. I perceive that, though you are very smart, whatever your boy-love asserts, however he says things are, you can't bear to contradict him – you change up and down. So too in the Assembly, if you say something and the Athenian *demos* says it isn't so, you turn around and say whatever they want ... "

And Socrates then picks the four greatest Athenian statesmen of the fifth century – Themistocles, Miltiades, Cimon, Pericles[16] – and has the brass to say that they were no better than the current crop of demagogues, indeed worse: those giants were more servile (δια-κονικώτεροι, 517B) than are the shrimps who lead us now. That this judgment is harshly biased, intemperate in the extreme, should not pass unnoticed: see Thucydides on Pericles as a corrective (2.65.8). Nor should we fail to notice that Socrates is represented as airing his ferocious critiques of Athens in very public contexts. In the *Gorgias* he has a considerable audience: Gorgias' Athenian clique has turned out in force along with many others. In the *Apology* there are 501 jurors and who knows how many hundred others in the audience. Socrates advertises sentiments which in the mind of malicious (or even merely thoughtless) hearers would more than suffice to convict

---

[16] *G.* 515C–516E. That the selection of these names cuts across party lines has often been noticed. Cimon, the staunch conservative, friend of Sparta, flanks Pericles, his archrival, the architect of ἄκρα δημοκρατία, Aristotle's *bête noire*.

him of oligarchic partisanship. Much less would have sufficed to tar him with this brush. Isocrates, who had done no more to bait the superdemocrats than advocate a return to the conservative democracy which his fancy locates in Athens' earlier history, says he had been warned that

T9 Isocr. *Areop.* 57: "I ran the risk, even while giving you the best advice, of being thought an enemy of the people (*misodēmos*) and of seeking to turn the city into an oligarchy."

But let us not lose track of the main point in the present argument. The question is whether or not, in putting into Socrates' mouth those bitter attacks on Athens' political life in the *Apology* and the *Gorgias*, Plato is undermining the credibility of his assurance in the *Crito* that Socrates finds the constitution of Athens "exceedingly pleasing" to him and prefers it to that of "any other city, Greek or barbarian." The answer, surely, is that he is not. Certainly there is no *contradiction*. If I believe that the laws of city A are better than those of city B, I incur no inconsistency in saying that city B observes its laws more faithfully than does city A. There is nothing wrong with A's laws, I might explain; the fault lies with the people who abuse them. This is the view Socrates takes of the wrong done to him by the jury that condemned him. At the conclusion of the discourse of the laws in the *Crito*, they say to him:

T10 *Cr.* 54B–C: "You will depart, wronged not by us, the laws, but by men."

For the wrong of his condemnation Socrates blames men, not Athenian law. This is not because he thinks that law perfect (cf. *Ap.* 37A7–B1), but because he thinks it a reasonable law under which fair-minded judges could and should have acquitted him. By the same token he could have held that the innocent people who were terrorized by political blackmailers ("sycophants") in Athens are wronged by men, not by laws, and that when Athenian politicians betray the high trust of their office by resort to flattery, it is their personal depravity, not that of the law, which is to blame: if they had true integrity they would rather die than flatter.

Thus neither in the *Apology* nor in the *Gorgias* – nor, I may add, anywhere in Plato's Socratic dialogues – does Socrates rescind that personal vote of confidence he gives the Athenian constitution in the

Crito. If we were to agree with Burnet that Socrates is "an uncompromising opponent of the Periclean democracy" (1914:188), with Heinrich Maier that for Socrates "democracy is the most perverse of all forms of government" (1913:417), with W. K. C. Guthrie that Socrates held views which "contravened the whole basis of democracy as then understood at Athens" (1969:410), we would have to do so in defiance of Plato's testimony. To support such views we would have to look exclusively to Xenophon.[17]

Our star passage would be the following:

T11 Xenophon, *Mem.* 3.9.10: "He said that kings and rulers are not those who hold the scepter, nor those elected by chance persons nor those who owe their power to force or deception; but those who know how to rule. For once it was granted that it is of the ruler to order what should be done and for the ruled to obey, he proceeded to point out that on a ship he who has knowledge is the ruler, while the ship-owner and all others on board obey the one who has knowledge [and so too in the case of farming, treatment of the sick, physical training, wool-spinning: those who have knowledge rule]."

Xenophon is adverting here to Socrates' cardinal doctrine that knowledge "is"[18] virtue, taking it to have a direct political import, which he understands as follows: there is a form of knowledge whose possession is as necessary a qualification for serving as ruler in a polis as is knowledge of navigation for being the captain of a ship or

---

[17] A quick look at the textual evidence these scholars cite for those opinions will show that, with but one exception, all of it comes from Xenophon. The exception is *Pr.* 319c–D: having just pointed out that when some technical topic is up for consideration before the Assembly, only expert testimony is welcome, Socrates proceeds: "But when there is need to deliberate about public policy, a builder will get up to advise or a coppersmith or a cobbler, a merchant, an importer, rich or poor, of high or low birth, and no one rebukes him, as in the former case, for offering advice without having acquired any knowledge or ever having had a teacher. Clearly, they think that [this sort of knowledge] cannot be taught."

To find in this remark "cruel scorn for the whole of Athenian democracy" (Maier, 1913: 418, n. 1) one would have to read into it the anti-democratic animus which Xenophon imputes to Socrates. Otherwise there would be nothing in the text to indicate that the procedure here described is absurd or even the least bit unreasonable. Consider the debate on Mytilene (Thuc. 3.36ff.) and the ones that followed on Torone, Scione, and Melos, as the war dragged on. One can hardly imagine a question of greater moral urgency than genocide as an instrument of imperial policy. If the Athenians believed that moral expertise were available for consultation, Plato's Socrates (*Cr.* 47A–48A) would insist that this, and this alone, should decide the issue. Believing as they do that it is unavailable, why should he think it unreasonable of them to open it up for discussion by everyone who is to share in moral responsibility for the decision?

[18] The precise import of the copula in this classical formula is a topic for a separate investigation. For my purposes in the present chapter it suffices to give it its minimal sense, that of necessary interentailment: all those who have virtue necessarily have knowledge and vice versa.

knowledge of agriculture for serving as the manager of a productive farm. This knowledge, which Socrates calls "the royal art,"[19] is the sine qua non of political authority; a ruler who lacks it is a fake; his authority has no legitimacy. What is the political[20] content of this art – what is it knowledge *of*? That it is knowledge of ruling is uninformatively tautologous. What we need to learn is what the ruler must know in order to know how to rule. Though there is no direct answer to this in Xenophon, we can derive it from what we learn there of Socrates' view of the quintessential attribute of the good ruler. On this Xenophon is very clear:

T12 *Mem.* 3.2.4: "When [Socrates] inquired what is the virtue of a good ruler, he stripped away everything but this: making his followers happy."

And how Xenophon understands Socrates' conception of the happiness (*eudaimonia*) which the good ruler procures for his subjects we can see no less clearly in the analysis of the function of a citizen which Xenophon puts into Socrates' mouth, i.e. of what each citizen would contribute to the city if his civic activities were well directed:

T13 *Mem.* 4.6.14: "Let us inquire what is the function of a good citizen. In the administration of moneys is not the superior citizen he who makes the city richer? ... In war, is it not he who makes her prevail over her enemies? ... In embassies, he who makes friends for her in lieu of enemies? ... In public oratory, he who allays civic strife and produces harmony?"

Thus what Socrates takes to be the elements of civic happiness, according to Xenophon, are material affluence, military supremacy, good relations with other cities, good relations among the citizens themselves. These are the things the ruler must know himself if he is

---

[19] He tells young Euthydemus, aspirant to political leadership in Athens: "You desire that excellence through which men become πολιτικοί and οἰκονομικοί and capable of ruling and being useful both to others and to themselves ... You desire the noblest excellence and the greatest art, for it belongs to kings and is called 'royal'" (*Mem.* 4.2.11).

[20] For its *moral* content see especially the dialogue with Aristippus, *Mem.* 2.1. In the "royal art" (2.1.17) the latter sees a rule of life which inures men to that disciplined endurance of hardship and sacrifice of gratification through which one earns one's place in the master-class. Thus the moral component of the "royal art" is that characteristic Xenophontic virtue, ἐγκράτεια, which, according to Xenophon, Socrates considers the "foundation (κρηπίδα) of all virtue" (*Mem.* 1.5.4: cf. 2.1.1 and 4.5.1; in Plato's Socratic dialogues ἐγκράτεια is never singled out as a special virtue on a par with the canonical five – the word ἐγκράτεια never occurs in the Socratic dialogues, only the adjective ἐγκρατής [once, in its commonplace use, *G.* 491D]).

to direct his subjects' efforts towards their attainment. He must have knowledge of the various branches of statecraft – of public finance, of military science, of the arts of diplomacy, of the rhetoric of civic amity.[21]

Would Athenian democracy pass muster when inspected from this point of view? Its most distinctive political institution, election by lot, would suffice to damn it. Judged as a device to snag for the offices of the polis those and only those who possess the "royal art," election by lot would strike anyone as the "silly" thing Polycrates had charged and Xenophon had conceded Socrates thought it to be, as we saw in T4 above. One might try to extenuate the offense of democracy to the "royal art" by arguing that those elected by this device were the magistrates – subordinate officers of the administration. But this would overlook the fact that not only they were elected by lot. So was the Council – the probouleutic and executive committee of the sovereign Assembly. And so were all the dicasteries, whose supreme judicial authority was on a par with that of the sovereign Assembly. Aristotle underlines the significance of their power:

T14 Aristotle, *Ath. Pol.* 9.1:   When the people have sovereignty in the voting [in the courts], they become sovereign in the constitution.

To be sure, for the appointment of the generals – the most important executive officers of the state – Athens resorted to an alternative procedure which it shared with the oligarchies: election by show of hands in the Assembly. In the eyes of Xenophon's Socrates this would be a redeeming feature – but not redeeming enough, given his low opinion of the intellectual level of the democratic electorate. This is how he talks about it when trying to persuade his friend Charmides to speak before the Assembly:

T15 Xenophon, *Mem.* 3.7. 5–6:   "You speak unabashed and unintimidated in the company of the most intelligent and capable people, and yet you are scared to speak in the company of the feeblest and most stupid. Of whom are you

---

[21] Attaching supreme importance to the first two (to both of them in conjunction, for he takes them to be closely interconnected: see the dialogue with Nicomachides, *Mem.* 3.4), Socrates enjoins expertise in them to those who hold high office in Athens or who aspire, or should aspire, to it: to Pericles' son, now general (*Mem.* 3.5), to Glaucon (3.6), to Charmides (3.7). In marked contrast to the Socrates depicted in Plato's Socratic dialogues, Xenophon's Socrates appears to be highly expert in public finance and military science: he is in a position to offer detailed advice in these areas to Pericles and to Glaucon (*Mem.* 3.5–6).

frightened? The fullers, cobblers, builders, coppersmiths, farmers, merchants and those who traffic in the market, caring for nothing but to buy cheap and sell dear – for it is from all these that the Assembly is made up."

This is not formal doctrine. But it reveals clearly enough what Xenophon takes to be Socrates' attitude to the working classes of Athens: to the people who make up the great bulk of the Assembly he refers as "the feeblest and most stupid" members of the civic body. In another well-known passage we see how, according to Xenophon, Socrates feels about that largest single segment of the working population which he calls *"banausoi"* – a highly emotive term which no one would apply to them to their face, unless one wanted to insult them:

T16 Xenophon, *Oeconomicus* 4.2:   "The so-called 'banausic' occupations are badly spoken of and, quite naturally, are held in utter contempt in our cities. For they ruin the bodies of those who work in them and of their foremen, forcing them into sedentary indoor work. And as their bodies become woman-ish their souls too become much more debilitated. Moreover these so-called banausic crafts allow no leisure for attention to one's friends and to the city, so that such people are thought bad both in dealing with friends and in defending their fatherland. And in some cities, particularly those which are good in war, citizens are not even allowed to work in banausic crafts." (Cf. also *Oec.* 6.4–9.)

Bypassing the folkloric psychophysiology of the supposed effects of indoor, sedentary work on the body and therewith on the soul, let us concentrate on the remark that banausic occupations allow no *leisure*. Xenophon's Socrates thinks of them as closing off to the *banausos* that area in which the upper-class Greek locates the intrinsically worthwhile activities of his life – music and poetry, sport, friendship, politics. We can see in Aristotle where this line of thought takes us when pushed further by a powerful thinker. It divides the population of the polis into the "necessary" people, as Aristotle calls them, and the "beautiful" people, the "worthwhile" people (*kaloi kagathoi, chrestoi*), as they like to call themselves. It follows that when the purpose of the polis is conceived in the Greek way – to realize the good life for its citizens – civic status should be limited, so far as possible, to the beautiful people, and should include as few as possible of the necessary ones:

T17 Aristotle, *Pol.* 1278a8–13:   The best polis will not make the *banausos* a citizen. But if he too is to be a citizen, then what we previously said was the citizen's virtue will not be for everyone – for every freeman – but only for those who are exempt from the necessary services which slaves perform for individuals, *banausoi* and *thētes* for the public.

This is the most fundamental point on which democrats and oligarchs divide. Democracy stands for inclusive citizenship – inclusive of *banausoi*: all Athenians born of native Athenians are citizens of Athens. Oligarchy stands for exclusive citizenship – exclusive of *banausoi*, so far as possible:[22] of all Thebans born of native Thebans half or less would be citizens of Thebes.[23] If Socrates had advocated disfranchisement of the *banausoi* – which would have cut Athens' civic rolls by nearly half – he would have declared openly for oligarchy. Given Xenophon's apologetic interests, his Socrates cannot be allowed to go so far. But no doubt is left in the reader's mind where Socrates' preference would lie: if the *banausoi* have civic status they will swarm into the Council and the dicasteries through the lot; they will have the swing-vote there as in the sovereign Assembly; the fate of "the most intelligent and capable" members of the civic body – the only ones who, by the doctrine of the "royal art," should have any access at all to political office – will be at the mercy of the judgment of the "feeblest and most stupid," entrusted to them by the operation of the lot. In the Socrates of Xenophon's Socratic writings, upon the one hand, and of Plato's Socratic dialogues, on the other, we meet two philosophers whose political sentiments are diametrically opposite. The convictions of Xenophon's Socrates commit him to an overwhelming preference for oligarchy over democracy. Plato's Socrates, though harshly critical of lawless and unjust conduct in the city of his birth, nonetheless prefers the constitution of

---

[22] Phormisius' proposal to restrict citizenship to those who owned land, which would have disfranchised no more than 5,000 – approximately a quarter of the civic body (sadly depleted by the preceding civil war) strikes the highborn Athenian who opposes it as expressing the sentiments of those "who in their heart were with the men of the city [the oligarchs who supported the Thirty] and only by accident found themselves on the side of the men of Peiraeus [the democrats under Thrasybulus]" (Lysias, *Or.* 34.2).

[23] In an earlier study ("*Isonomia Politikē*," first published in 1964, reprinted in *PS* 164ff. at 179, nn. 63–4) I allow that the figure might be slightly higher than 50%, noting, however, that ps.-Herodes, *Peri Politeias* (30–1) "gives the 1:3 ratio of active citizens to the rest [of the native population] as the smallest in the oligarchies established by Sparta (at the end of the Peloponnesian War)." Ostwald, 1969: 118, nn. 3 and 5, favors the 1:3 ratio and is cited as the authority for that figure in Demand, 1982: 16 with n. 4. Moore, 1975: 129, opts for a higher figure: "a little under half the population would have had full rights."

that city – the most extreme democracy of his world – to that of every other state known to him, including that of each of the "well-governed" oligarchies he names.

Here I must face a powerful argument – so powerful that if I could not produce a completely adequate reply the whole of the foregoing argument would be gutted: "But does not Plato's Socrates *also* hold the doctrine of the 'royal art'? Would not this have the same anti-democratic import?" The answer, in a nutshell, is that Plato's Socrates most certainly has *a* doctrine of the "royal art"; but it is not the same doctrine and has no anti-democratic import. To see why this is so we must go down to the rock-bottom of Socrates' moral philosophy, the thesis that virtue is knowledge, and face up to the fact that the knowledge Socrates has in view in Plato's Socratic dialogues is *exclusively moral knowledge*: it has nothing to do with knowledge of the instrumentalities of the good life; it is knowledge of ends or, more precisely, knowledge of *the* end of the good life, that unique end which is for Plato's Socrates, unlike Xenophon's, the only thing which matters: the perfection of the soul, its moral perfection, on which, for Plato's Socrates, human happiness depends:

T18 *G.* 470E8–11: Polus: "What? Is the whole of happiness in that (sc. *paideia* and justice)?" Socrates: "Yes, Polus, that is what I say. For I say that the noble and good man and woman is happy, the unjust and wicked wretched."

Every non-moral good – wealth, health, honor, pleasure, life itself – is immaterial for human happiness. Each of these goods is worthless in and of itself (*Eud.* 281D–E); each of them may be evil instead of good unless we know how to use it in the service of moral improvement:

T19 *Eud.* 288E7–289B2: "Even if we knew how to turn stones into gold, such knowledge would be worthless. For if we did not know how to use gold, it would profit us nothing ... Even if there were some knowledge that would make us immortal, if we did not know how to use our immortality, even that would profit us nothing ..."

This being as true for our corporate as for our private life, the knowledge which should direct the city is the same as that which should direct each individual man and woman: knowledge of the end, the same end, perfection of soul. Hence the criterion of good statesmanship is ability to assist the people of the city – all of them, not just those who have leisure for the amenities – all the citizens, including, of course, the *banausoi*, and all the non-citizens as well: everyone in the city, including the slaves. This, Callicles is told in the *Gorgias*, is how his excellence as a statesman should be judged:

T20 *G.* 515A4–7: "Say, has Callicles made any citizen a better man? Is there anyone, citizen or alien, freeman or slave, formerly wicked – unjust, dissolute, intemperate – who has become a good and noble man because of Callicles?"

Can we imagine what a transvaluation of values this Socrates – Plato's, not Xenophon's – presses on his world in telling an upper-class Athenian that the criterion of his statesmanship is whether or not it improves the souls of the people of Athens – even the souls of *slaves*?[24] In this conception of human virtue the distinction between the "necessary" and the "beautiful" people is wiped out. There are no second-class souls.

This is the knowledge – soul-perfecting knowledge – which Plato's Socrates calls "the political art" and "the royal art": the phrases are the same as in Xenophon but their content is radically different, for in Plato they *exclude* those very competences which, as we saw above,[25] are at the heart of the "royal art" for Socrates in Xenophon:

T21 *Eud.* 292B4–C1: "As for those other things which might be said to belong to the political art [= the royal art: 291B4ff.] – and they are many, e.g. to make the citizens rich, free [sc. from external domination], undisturbed by faction: *these things have turned out to be neither good nor evil*, while what the citizens need, if they are to be benefited and made happy, is to be made wise – to have [moral] knowledge imparted to them."

For Xenophon's Socrates the royal art is statecraft – mastery of the great instrumentalities of civic happiness: wealth, military supremacy, good external relations, harmonious internal relations. For Plato's Socrates the royal art is nothing of that sort. It has no more to do with the art of fiscal prudence, of military science, of shrewd diplomacy, of persuasive oratory, than with the art of making us

---

[24] See also the similar description of the teacher whose mission is to care for souls in the *Laches* (186B): to qualify one should be able to show "which Athenians or aliens, slaves or freemen, have become admittedly good men because of him."

[25] Note the place of the οἰκονομικός in the description of the "royal art" in *Mem.* 4.2.11, cited in n. 19 above. Both economic and military science are prime qualifications for those who are, or should be, holding high political office: n. 21 above.

immortal or of turning stones into gold.[26] Needless to say, we cannot run a city without economists, generals, ambassadors, orators, and other masters of the instrumentalities: public doctors, architects, engineers, and so forth. But all these specialists should do their job under the direction of the royal art, whose sole competence is moral knowledge: expertise in determining how the instrumentalities of statecraft can be used best in the interest of moral perfection.[27]

This wisdom cannot be monopolized by members of the city's upper crust, as it has to be for Xenophon's Socrates, for if it were, moral virtue could only belong to few, while for Plato's Socrates it must belong to everyone: everyone is called upon to make perfection of soul the supreme concern of his or her personal existence – everyone, alien and citizen, slave and freeman, female and male. This is the conviction which turns Plato's Socrates – not Xenophon's – into a street philosopher, which no philosopher had been before him and none would be after him, except perhaps the Cynics, and they only as his spiritual grandchildren: Socrates begat Antisthenes and Antisthenes begat Diogenes the Dog. The call "perfect your soul" goes out to everyone, delivered personally by Plato's Socrates to "anyone he runs into" in the market or on the street:

T22 *Ap.* 29D–30A: "I shall not cease philosophizing and exhorting you and expostulating with each one of you I happen to run into, saying to him in my customary way: 'O best of men, Athenian, citizen of the greatest city, most highly reputed for its wisdom and power, are you not ashamed to be concerned to make as much money as possible and for reputation and prestige, while for wisdom and truth and for the greatest possible improvement of your soul you have no care or worry?' ... These things I will say to anyone I run into, young or old, alien or citizen ... "

The conception of the royal art which Xenophon ascribes to Socrates is *oligarchic* in the literal sense of that word: in principle, it

---

[26] As is clear at T21, even the appeasement of civic strife – to which Socrates might be expected to attach direct moral importance – is excluded from the scope of the royal art.

[27] "To this art both the general's and the other arts [of the economist, doctor, *et al.*: 289A5–6] turn over their several products to be governed by it, since only it knows how to use them" (*Eud.* 291C7–9). The notion that this art should do the work of the general, economist, and the like, is debunked in the deceitful fantasy ("dream of ivory") in the *Ch.* (173A–D) where moral wisdom (σωφροσύνη) is given the job of ensuring that the various craftsmen ("doctor, general, or anyone else" [173B2–3]) should do their work with technical competence (τεχνικῶς): if, *per impossibile*, the job were done, we would still not know if, as a result, "we would do well and would be happy" (173D4).

belongs only to *few* – those few who have had the leisure and other opportunities to acquire knowledge of statecraft – assuring them that, in virtue of their possession of that knowledge, they and they alone are the legitimate rulers of the city. Should I say that the conception of that art which Plato ascribes to Socrates is *demo*cratic in the same literal sense – it belongs to the *demos*? No, for that would *under*state its scope: it is for every person, including all those who did not belong to the Athenian *demos* – aliens no less than citizens, slaves no less than freemen, women no less than men.[28] All are invited to seek it. But who, if any, will come to possess it remains in doubt. So my argument should hew strictly to the terms of my second thesis, whose limited scope should not be missed.

Let me remind you of the terms in which I formulated that thesis at the start: the perception of Socrates as a crypto-oligarch is a misperception. And let me recall the way I sized up the import of the positive evidence for that thesis I have offered in this chapter – the only positive evidence for it there is: the three texts in the *Crito*. There Socrates declares his personal preference for the constitution of his native city – the most democratic constitution the mind of man had yet conceived. But he produces no theory to justify that preference – not even the adumbration of a theory. The word "democracy" is never mentioned. The preference is expressed without naming, or describing, the form of government it represents, so *a fortiori* without producing, or even suggesting, a rationale for that preference. When I came to the conception of good statesmanship which is expressed by his use of the phrase "the royal art," I contrasted it sharply with the use of the same phrase by Xenophon's Socrates, pointing out that while the latter is a *political* doctrine in the strict sense of the term (it stipulates the conditions of legitimacy of the tenure of political power), the former is properly speaking a *moral* doctrine: it defines only the moral dimension of the statesman's vocation. That this moral doctrine has far-reaching political *implications* is clear enough, since it obliterates the distinction between the beautiful people and the necessary people which was the moral basis

---

[28] Note the conjunction. "man and woman," in T18 above, For Socrates moral virtue is the same in women as in men (*Meno* 72D–73B).

for the disfranchisement of large segments of the working population in the oligarchies. This feature of Socrates' thought could be expressed in Greek by the term δημοτικός, used by orators and historians to designate the attitude of one who is well-disposed towards the people, who is φιλόδημος instead of μισόδημος. There is no proper counterpart to δημοτικός in English; the nearest we can come to it is by an extended use of "democratic." In that extended use of the term we can say that Socrates' conception of the "royal art" *is* democratic, though "demophilic" would be less misleading. The sentiment which it expresses in contrast to that conveyed by the use of the same phrase in Xenophon's account of Socrates may best be captured by projecting the two conceptions on an ideal plane: imagine that all our hopes for what is good, beautiful and sensible for men and women were fulfilled. Then, if we follow Xenophon's Socrates, the spirit and structure of that fair city's government would be profoundly oligarchic: the knowledge and vision of a privileged leisure class would rule the visionless multitude. Not so if we followed the Socrates of Plato's Socratic dialogues: there every one of us would have the royal art, each of us would pursue the "examined life," we would all be ruled in our individual lives by our personal knowledge and vision of the good. The business of government would be transacted for us, for our benefit, by hired technicians – economists, generals, diplomats, legal experts, and so on, appointed by us and responsible to us. These hirelings would be masters of statecraft.[29] This would be their unique qualification for office – *not* mastery of the royal art: this would belong no more to them than to the rest of us as the inalienable privilege of our pursuit of the life of virtue.

But what of the real Athens – the actual city, which no one, by any stretch of the imagination, could think might come to be ruled, under its present constitution, by wisdom directing every civic activity towards a single imperious end – perfection of soul? Did Socrates hold views subversive of "the established constitution,"[30] as those who prosecuted him and many of those who had voted against him

---

[29] This is what Socrates thinks the holders of governmental office should be: craftsmen hired to ply their craft for the exclusive benefit of the governed (*R.* I, 346E–347D).
[30] Cf. T4 above in conjunction with n. 14.

had believed? In this chapter I have offered evidence that contrary answers must be given to this question, depending on whether or not we are to believe Xenophon or Plato. If we believe Xenophon, our answer must be, "Yes, they were – profoundly so." The attack on election by lot would not of itself compel this answer. The lot was vulnerable to criticism on philodemic grounds. As we know from Isocrates, one could take pot-shots at it without surrendering one's claim to be a loyal democrat.[31] What would be fatal to that claim is the conviction that, in the phraseology of T11 above, only he who "knows how to rule" is a true "ruler," i.e. that entitlement to office is contingent on satisfying a condition which only a small minority of Athenians could hope to satisfy: expertise in statecraft comparable to that of accomplished craftsmen in the performing or productive arts. It would follow from this view that to randomize distribution of offices over a civic body in which "the feeblest and most stupid" (T15) greatly outnumber the capable and intelligent would be to ensure, by the laws of statistical probability, that the great majority of those offices would go to people whose tenure of office lacks legitimacy. The order of the magistrate would then have no authority unless ad hoc evidence were available that it proceeded on the requisite knowledge of statecraft. And the verdicts of the courts would have no authority, for who would want to argue that a majority of 201 or 501 or 1,001 lot-selected jurors were knowledgeable jurists? To save the legitimacy of Athenian government in the face of such a root-and-branch rejection of its procedures one might dredge up that curious bit of legal positivism in book IV of the *Memorabilia*[32] which, so surprisingly, identifies the just with the legal. But this would be unavailing. For Athenian positive law, made in the last analysis by lot-selected legislative commissions or by the sovereign Assembly, would itself lack authority, since in those bodies

---

[31] *Areop.* 23: Our ancestors thought election ἐκ προκρίτων "more favorable to the people (δημοτικωτέραν) than was sortition: under the latter chance would decide the issue and a partisan of oligarchy would often get the office ..." Elsewhere (*PS* 186–8, and nn. 87 and 88) I have argued against classifying Isocrates as a pro-oligarchic Athenian. A man whose proposed reforms, however reactionary, entail no disfranchisement of landless and banausic citizens and leave the *demos* with the sovereign power "to appoint the magistrates, punish misdemeanors and adjudicate disputes [i.e. with plenary elective and judicial powers]" (*Areop.* 26, and cf. *Panath.* 147), is *not* an advocate of oligarchy.

[32] *Mem.* 4.4.12: Socrates: "I say that what is legal (νόμιμον) is just." Hippias: "Socrates, do you mean that the legal and the just are the same?" Socrates: "I do."

those who do have knowledge of statecraft would be greatly out-
numbered by those who don't.

Not so, if we are to go by what we learn in Plato's earlier dialogues. While Socrates there repeatedly makes unforgivably intemperate allegations of wrongdoing in Athenian public life and attacks
pay for public office, whose effect on the character he considers
corrupting (*G.* 515E),[33] he never attacks any other Athenian institution, never says a word against election by lot, never says, or directly
implies, that knowledge of statecraft is a condition of legitimate civic
authority. He tells his friend in the privacy of his prison cell, where
he could have no motive for dissembling, that he prefers the laws of
Athens to those of any other state known to him. He does not
question the moral authority of the court which condemned him
even though he thinks its verdict most unjust. He gives morally
weighty reasons, consistent with all his other views, why every Athenian is morally obligated to obey every legal order by its officers
unless he considers it unjust, in which case he may protest its
injustice but must consent to punishment if his protest proves
unavailing.[34] Both in his doctrines and in his personal conduct
Plato's Socrates is profoundly and consistently loyal to the Athenian
constitution.

Who then is the true, historical, Socrates? Xenophon's or Plato's?
Which of the two I believe it is, you have already guessed. A declaration of faith on my part in this last gasp of the chapter would be
redundant. What you would like is not faith, but knowledge – even

---

[33] Though the attack is indirect (Pericles is reproached for having made the Athenians "idle
and cowardly and talkative and greedy, having been the first to establish pay for public
office"), it is clear enough and I do not wish to underestimate its importance. It warrants
the inference that his political sentiments were conservative – which would be entirely
consistent with the preference for democracy over oligarchy, as we know from the case of
Isocrates.

[34] *Cr.* 51B8–C1: "In war, in law-court, *everywhere*, one must do what one's city and fatherland
commands or persuade her as to the nature of justice." For the interpretation of this
much debated text I am indebted to Kraut (1981:6): "The citizen may disobey but only on
condition that he justify his act in an appropriate public forum ... The persuade-or-obey
doctrine is the Socratic analogue to the contemporary notion of conscientious refusal." The
case for Kraut's textual exegesis will be strengthened if we note that in the cited text the
verb πείθω, which comes through the translations as "persuade," is, unlike the latter, *not*
a "success-verb": thus Socrates in the *Apology* spends all day long "persuading" (30E7,
31B5) people whom he does not convince. If Socrates had believed that he was justified in
disobeying a legal command only if he had reasonable prospects of convincing a court of
law that the command was unjust, the effective scope of permissible disobedience would be
sadly reduced.

a few crumbs of it would be better than nothing, if richer fare were unavailable. If your demand were as modest as that, I could meet it. I can offer you two good-sized crumbs. We do know of two things which give us some reason for believing that the Socrates who preferred democracy to oligarchy is the true one.

The first is his association with Chaerephon, of whose strongly democratic partisanship there is no doubt. In 404 B.C., when the junta, supported by the Spartan occupational force, ruled Athens, Chaerephon fled to join the resistance under Thrasybulus and fought with that band which, under desperate odds, liberated Athens. Chaerephon had been "from youth" (*Ap.* 21A1) Socrates' friend, his ardent, devoted disciple: Aristophanes makes him Socrates' deputy, almost his equal, in the Thinkery.[35] What sense could be made of that, if Socrates had been a crypto-oligarch?

The second thing is that Socrates had kept the admiration of Lysias, whose identification with the democratic cause is also beyond doubt: it is manifest in the lavish aid Lysias had given from his own purse to the resistance movement and in the sentiments voiced in the speech he wrote for the Athenian who opposed the motion of Phormisius which, if passed, would have disfranchised 5,000 landless Athenians.[36] Lysias, who had known Socrates well, sprung to the defense of his memory in the debate that followed within a few years of his death, producing an *Apology* (schol. by Arethas on Plato, *Ap.* 18B), probably in rebuttal of Polycrates' *Accusation*, whose attack on Socrates had been strongly political. If Lysias had thought Socrates an enemy of the restored democracy, he could not have entered the lists on his behalf in that debate.

These wisps of inference give us some reason to believe that friends of Socrates, who staked their lives and fortunes on Athenian democracy at a time when its survival hung on a thread, had felt that Socrates was on their side.[37]

---

[35] For the references see Vlastos, 1980: 351.

[36] For the references see Vlastos, 1983d: 206.

[37] I want to record my gratitude to the Hastings Center for appointing me Senior Visiting Scholar during 1982–3. This essay is a partial outcome of studies in the philosophy of Socrates which my residence at the Center enabled me to pursue under ideally congenial and invigorating conditions.

5

THE *PROTAGORAS* AND THE *LACHES*

I MORAL VS. TECHNICAL KNOWLEDGE

There is a passage in the *Laches* which poses a problem for the
interpreter of Socrates' moral theory. Though often discussed in the
scholarly literature, there has been as yet no definitive solution to its
puzzle. It occurs in Socrates' argument with Laches 192D–193C.

The answer Laches had just proposed – "endurance"[1] – (192B–C)
to "What is courage?" had been rejected because it failed to stipu-
late that, to qualify as courageous, endurance had to be guided by
wisdom. Drop that stipulation and the answer is easily discredited:

TI *La.* 192C–D: "Is not wise endurance noble and good?" "Absolutely."
"And what of foolish endurance? Is not that, on the contrary, harmful and
evil?" "Yes." "And would you say that that sort of thing, evil and harmful, is
noble?" "That would not be right, Socrates." "So you would not consider it
courage, for it is not the noble thing which courage is?" "True." "So according
to this argument courage would be *wise* endurance?"

When Laches agrees – he could hardly do otherwise – it looks as
though Socrates would concede that *courage is wise endurance.* But
he does not. What he now wants to know is *what sort of wisdom* this
would have to be: "Wise in *what* (εἰς τί φρόνιμος)? In all things, be
they great or small?" he asks,[2] and then proceeds to cite case after
case of wise endurance whose wisdom gives us no reason to call it
courageous:

---

[1] Or "persistence," "perseverance," "steadfastness": καρτερία.
[2] 192E. He rephrases the question a little later (194E) as *"what sort* of knowledge (ποία
σοφία)?"

(1) A financier wisely perseveres in putting his money into something which he knows will prove a good investment.
(2) A doctor wisely persists in maintaining the regimen required for the patient's illness, unmoved by the latter's pleas to be allowed relief
(3) A military commander wisely persists in attacking an opposing force which he knows to be weaker than his own.
(4) A cavalryman, skilled in horsemanship, persists in doing battle against an opponent unskilled in that craft.[3]
(5) A peltast or bowman, skilled in his craft, persists in fighting against an opponent unskilled in that craft.
(6) An expert swimmer dives into a cistern more steadfastly than others who lack that expertise.

What is Socrates aiming to prove by these counter-examples to the proposal that courage is "wise endurance"? Is he welshing on the most famous of his moral doctrines which makes wisdom the hallmark of all the virtues, hence of courage no less than the rest? So some scholars have been tempted to think. That this is not what he intends is made immediately clear at the conclusion of the argument: he leads Laches to agree that "they did not speak well" in conceding that foolish endurance might count as courage (193D). So Laches – and Plato's reader – is left with an unresolved contradiction: courage is "wise endurance"; yet there are many cases in which a man who exhibits wise endurance gives us no reason to call him "brave": someone in the same circumstance enduring without wisdom strikes us as distinctly braver. How can this be?

The most attractive of the proposed solutions has been made by Santas, invoking the distinction between knowledge of fact and knowledge of value:

The cases that Socrates described for Laches contain information only on the first sort of knowledge, the agent's estimate of what the situation is and what are his chances of success; we are told nothing about how the agents

---

[3] A timely reminder: "wisdom" and "knowledge" are being used as synonyms throughout this passage as they are quite generally in the Socratic dialogues; and skill or know-how, no less than propositional knowledge, is counting as knowledge. Hence Socrates can speak without strain of a cavalryman's skill as "knowledge" or "wisdom" and of the opponent who lacks this skill as lacking in the relevant "wisdom."

conceived the values of that for the sake of which they were enduring and the values of the alternatives to enduring. But clearly information on these points will make a difference to our judgment whether the agent's endurance is wise or foolish. If, say, the man with the lesser or no advantage conceives what he is fighting for (say, the defense of his city) as high enough in value and/or the alternatives to enduring (say, the enslavement of his city and family) as low enough, his endurance in fighting on may be anything but foolish. (Santas, 1971: 193)

Clearly, this is true. If that distinction is applied systematically to the six cases Socrates had brought up, they will no longer count as counter-examples to the claim that "courage is wise endurance." The application is particularly illuminating in the sixth case:

To dive into a well, with no skill at diving, in order to save a child's life, when there is no one else to do it, is anything but foolishness. (Santas, 1971: 194)

Is this the solution we are looking for? What reason could we have to hesitate?

The reason is the fear of importing into our exegesis of Plato's thought a distinction, all too familiar in modern philosophy, which is never formulated in his own text. The fact – value contrast is never discussed, or even mentioned, as such in the Socratic dialogues. In fact, one wouldn't know how the exact counterpart of this contrast could be expressed in Greek. If we insist, as we should, on interpreting Socrates' thought only in terms indigenous to the terms in which it is expressed by himself, we must hesitate to have recourse to the fact – value contrast. Is there no alternative way of resolving the present difficulty? I believe that there is.

We can find it by paying close attention to the form of Socrates' question at 192E, "Knowledge concerning what? Of all things *be they great or small?*" and then recall that in the *Apology* Socrates had made entirely clear what it is that he rates the "great" and the "small" things in life: Anytus, he says, "could bring about my death, or exile, or deprivation of civic rights; he and others might think these great evils but I don't. Much greater is the evil he is doing now – undertaking to put someone unjustly to death" (30D). Here Socrates refuses to count any of those terrible harms which Anytus does have the power to inflict – deprivation of civic rights, exile, death – as "great" evils. Why? Because none of them would impair Socrates' virtue – none of them is a moral evil. What Socrates would count as a "great evil" is only that: the perpetration of an unjust deed, which Anytus has no power to make Socrates do. The same thought surfaces in the *Crito*: Socrates had remarked there that "if the many could do one the greatest evils, they should also have the power to do one the greatest goods; but in point of fact they can do neither" (44D). The "greatest evils" which "the many" do have the power to inflict are those which involve non-moral goods – the deprivation of material possessions, civic status, physical life. The "greatest goods" which they cannot confer are in the moral domain: they are impotent to make one morally better or worse: Socrates' virtue is beyond the power of the "many" to enhance or impair.

Following up this clue in our passage in the *Laches*, we can see that none of the goods exemplified in the six counter-examples – financial gain, physical health, military success, adeptness in diving into wells, or in peltastry, or fighting on horseback – would count as "great": none of them involves the enhancement of the agent's virtue; none of them is a moral good. So we can see that by "knowledge concerning great things" Socrates understands only what we would reckon *moral* knowledge in pointed contrast to the *technical* knowledge possessed by the people exemplified in each of the six cases he mentions. The "wisdom" in each of the latter is skill in obtaining things which Socrates would decline to count as "great" goods. In Aristotle's more highly developed vocabulary, a special term – "cleverness" (δεινότης) – is reserved for proficiency in such matters as these. In Plato's Socratic dialogues, indeed in the whole of his corpus, neither this term nor any equivalent to it is reserved for this purpose[4]. Moreover, Aristotle has a special term for "moral": moral wisdom he could identify as ἠθικὴ σοφία. Socrates has to manage without this term or any equivalent to it. How then is he going to cope with the problem which is as urgent in his own moral theory as in Aristotle's – the distinction between moral and non-moral wis-

---

[4] At *La.* 193C δεινός is, in fact, used to express technical skill: unskilled swimmers are said to dive into wells μὴ ὄντες δεινοί. But this occurs only for the nonce. δεινός is not reserved for this use. Socrates would have been as likely to express the same thought by saying μὴ ὄντες σοφοί.

dom[5] – between wise choice of moral ends and practical astuteness
in devising means to the attainment of morally unweighted ends?

We can see how he does the job in the *Apology* and the *Crito*, on
one hand, in the *Laches*, on the other. In both of the former dialogues
he uses the "great" goods/evils phrase to refer to moral goods/evils
in pointed contrast to the non-moral goods/evils which he reckons
"small." So when he refers to "wisdom" in these dialogues he could
only mean moral wisdom. In the *Laches* his procedure is more devious. To show that the claim "courage is wise endurance" is untouched by the counter-examples he selects the latter exclusively
from the domain of practical skills – the financier's, the doctor's,
the general's, the diver's, the peltast's, the cavalryman's. If it had
dawned on Laches that the goods such people can procure would
count as anything but "great," he would have seen that his proposal that courage is wise endurance was proof against the counter-
examples.

The reader might ask at this point if in the interpretation I am
proposing Socrates would be expecting altogether too much from
this interlocutor. Would it be reasonable to think that a military
man unschooled in philosophical argument could be expected to see
for himself the difference between the "small" things involved in the
wisdom of financiers, doctors, and the rest, and the "great" things at
stake in the wisdom of the man who knows that he is duty-bound
to stay at his post, accepting the imminent risk to life and limb?
The point is moot. Certainly here exceptionally severe demands are
made on the interlocutor's capacity to figure out for himself, without
direct help from Socrates, a vital truth of moral philosophy. But that
Laches fails so miserably to rise to this demand does not prove that
the demand was unreasonable. On Socrates' side it may be said that
if Laches had some perception, however vague, of the difference in
the wisdom deployed, on one hand, in buying cheap and selling

---

[5] Even in English, where "wisdom" commonly carries heavier moral freight than it does in
Greek, we use "wise" freely in the case of actions to which no moral evaluation is being
applied, as in an agriculturist's "wise" rotation of crops or in the "wise" distribution of
stresses and strains in a civil engineer's design. We even apply the term to the skillful choice
of means to the pursuit of ends we view as downright evil: an unscrupulous politician's
"wise" tactics in a campaign, or a shady financier's "wise" take-over of a rival company.

dear, in treating physical ailments, and the like, and that in standing
by the call of virtue at any cost to one's life and limb, on the
other, he would not have hesitated for a moment when asked,
"Knowledge in all things, both great and small?" He would have re-
plied, "Knowledge of the great things, the very greatest, Socrates."
To miss this cue was to betray that he really did not understand the
import of "wise" in "*wise* endurance": in thinking that he did know
he was self-deceived, a victim of the conceit of knowledge.

Let me now turn to two other dialogues where Socrates is more
forthcoming in help to an interlocutor faced with the same problem.
In the *Charmides* when Critias makes knowledge the critical term in
the definition of "temperance" (σωφροσύνη), the virtue under investigation there, Socrates presses him: the temperate person acts
"knowledgeably concerning what (τίνος ἐπιστημόνως)?" As we have
seen, this is the same question he had put to Laches. But here it is
followed up by ancillary questions which point more forcefully to the
correct answer: "Is it knowledge of cobbling? ... Or of work in
copper? ... Or work in wool, or anything else of that sort?" (*Ch.*
173D–E). Clearly not: it cannot be knowledge displayed in the in-
dustrial crafts because, as Critias had previously agreed, having this
kind of knowledge would not begin to ensure its possessor's happiness. To underline the significance of just this point Socrates had
resorted in the immediately preceding page to an elaborate device
unprecedented in the elenctic dialogues: a kind of "thought-experi-
ment"[6] couched in a philosophical fantasy he calls a "dream."

He had conjured up an imaginary world in which everyone knows
how to detect the difference between honest and fake workmanship
in the practical arts and crafts – which he takes to include not only
the cobbler's and the copper-worker's but even such exalted arts as
the general's and even the prophet's, credited ad hoc with unfail-
ingly reliable knowledge of the future. In such a world no imposture
would succeed in deceiving. All its work would be done with honesty
and impeccable efficacy. Doctors would always succeed in healing,
pilots would always navigate safely, generals always deploy optimally effective tactics. Blessed with such pervasive knowledge of the

---

[6] As Frerejohn, 1984: 113, has felicitously called it.

crafts and practical arts in that sort of world, would it follow that we would be happy? This we have been unable to learn, Socrates insists (173A–D). Critias, still resisting, replies, "But if you denigrate knowledge, you will not easily find the crown of happiness in anything else." He has missed the point (or is pretending to have missed it): Socrates had done nothing to denigrate knowledge as such. What he had done was bring home the truth that one sort of knowledge – technical mastery of the instrumentalities of life – cannot be the sort of knowledge in terms of which temperance (or any other virtue) may be defined, if it is agreed that virtue ensures our happiness.

He makes the same point in even stronger terms in the transitional dialogue, the *Euthydemus*. Here he gives wisdom a kind of apotheosis. He declares it (281E) the only thing that is good "itself by itself," for its goodness is not dependent on its conjunction with some other good, while in the case of all other goods their value is entirely dependent on their conjunction with wisdom, since only if they are wisely used would any of these other things be worth having at all: unwisely used they would be more of a liability than an asset for our happiness. The question what sort of knowledge this wisdom would have to be is raised again as, previously, in the *Laches* and the *Charmides*. And here Socrates marks it off by setting it in even more dramatic contrast to practical know-how than he had done in any previous dialogue. He fabricates examples of technical knowledge which fantasticate its efficacy: he dreams up (288E–289B) the power to change stones into gold or to make ourselves immortal. Supposing we did have such abilities as these, he insists, in the absence of wisdom they would be worthless: if we did not know how to make the right use of our fabulous heaps of gold or of our immortality, they "would profit us nothing" (289A), for they would not ensure our happiness. The wisdom needed for this would differ as radically from these as from any of the other practical crafts, for only this – knowing how to use whatever goods technical wisdom might procure for us – could make us happy.

Let us look back at the results reached so far: three Socratic dialogues – the *Laches*, the *Charmides*, and the *Euthydemus* – confront a problem which every moral theory must address: the difference between, on one hand, the wisdom required for the morally wise choice of ends and, on the other, for devising optimally effective means to morally unweighted ends. If, like Aristotle, Socrates had hit on different words to name the different sorts of wisdom involved in each of the two cases – "moral wisdom" in the first, "cleverness" in the second – he would have had from the first a ready handle on the problem. In the *Laches* he would have easily disarmed the counter-examples by categorizing their know-how as "cleverness" whose possession is irrelevant to the kind of wisdom required for courage as for each of the other virtues. Lacking that very useful term he offers the interlocutor no greater help than the initial hint that this kind of wisdom concerns "great" things, resting content after that with marshalling an array of non-moral skills hoping that this will of itself suggest the intended contrast. In the *Charmides* he does considerably better: he identifies the wisdom he has in view as knowledge which makes us happy; and he uses the "dream" to help the interlocutor realize that unlimited success in the area of the arts and crafts could not begin to ensure happiness. In the *Euthydemus* he hits on a parallel differentia of the wisdom which itself constitutes the sovereign good in human life: it is the unique knowledge which vouchsafes the ability to make right use of every other good.

Now let us look at the *Protagoras*. The "power of knowledge" (352A–C) is the central thesis of this wide-ranging, sprawling dialogue. Socrates intimates to his interlocutor that if they can agree on this their outstanding differences will be resolved. And Protagoras does agree – much too hastily, without pondering the consequences of agreement on this point for other beliefs of his which he considers matters of common experience and common sense: he will have to agree that having the knowledge Socrates has in view will entail possession of all the moral virtues, which strikes him as patently false: surely, he thinks, people sadly deficient in such knowledge may nonetheless be exceedingly brave (349D). This is the sticking point. Socrates had thought he could easily dislodge Protagoras from it with the brisk argument at 349E–350C which is premised on the claim that those who have the knowledge required for diving into wells, for cavalry warfare, and for peltastry and bowmanship, are made more confident by such know-how and *are, therefore,* braver than those who lack it.[7]

Coming to this argument fresh from the passage in the *Laches* with which the present essay began, one gets the surprise of one's life. The identical examples – expert divers, skilled cavalrymen, and skilled peltasts and bowmen (*Pr.* 350A) – which are used in the *Protagoras* in support of the superior courage of those who have technical expertise are used in the *Laches*, as we have seen, to establish the contrary thesis, sc. that people who endure danger though lacking expertise in diving, horsemanship, and peltastry are acting no less bravely than are experts in these crafts enduring the same danger. Plato could hardly have introduced the same three examples in the *Laches* unless he were deliberately contrasting the position he gives Socrates here with the one allowed him in the *Protagoras*. I submit that the simplest explanation of this fact is an advance in moral insight in Plato's own understanding of the true intent of the Socratic conception of courage as wisdom: when Plato has come to write the *Laches* he has seen clearly what he had not yet seen when he wrote the *Protagoras* – that the wisdom which accounts for the brave man's courage has everything to do with moral insight, *and nothing to do with technical skill.*

II   THE TERMINAL ARGUMENT IN THE *LACHES*[8]

A still sharper contrast in the teaching of the two dialogues awaits us in the closing pages of the *Laches*.[9] Here we see Socrates setting out to refute the definition of "courage" he had produced in the *Protagoras* and had used there with lethal effect against his adversary. I shall offer, first of all, an analysis of the structure of the argument in the *Laches* which exhibits it as a perfectly valid refutation of its target and shall then proceed to defend the soundness of

---

[7] In Vlastos, 1956: xxxii I followed this reading of 350C2–4 (οἱ σοφώτατοι οὗτοι καὶ θαρραλεώτατοί εἰσιν, θαρραλεώτατοι δὲ ὄντες ἀνδρειότατοι) and I still think that only on such a reading of these difficult lines can a logically valid argument be salvaged from the passage. I note that it is still being followed in Taylor, 1976: 44.

[8] It will be convenient to refer to this argument by the acronym "the *TAL.*"

[9] 197E–199E.

this analysis against an alternative one which, if true, would spirit away this contrast between the two dialogues.

(A)   Analysis of the argument[10]

(1)   Courage is knowledge of fearful and confidence-sustaining things (199A10–B1; cf. 194E11–195A1, 196D1–2). (Premise)

(2)   Courage is a part of virtue (198A1–9; cf. 190C8–D5). (Premise)

(3)   Fearful things are expected evils, confidence-sustaining things are expected goods (198B5–10). (Premise)

(4)   Expected evils/goods are future evils/goods (198B5–9). (Premise)

(5)   Fearful things are future evils; confidence-sustaining things are future goods (198C2–4). (From 3 and 4)

(6)   Courage is knowledge of future goods and evils (198C2–7; 199B3–4). (From 1 and 5)

(7)   Knowledge of future good and evil is the same as knowledge of all good and evil, be it future, present, or past (198D–199A). (Premise)

(8)   Courage is the same as the knowledge of all good and evil (199C–D). (From 6 and 7)

(9)   Knowledge of all good and evil is not a part of virtue but the whole of it (199D4–E4). (Premise)

(10)   Courage is not a part of virtue but the whole of it (199E6–9). (From 8 and 9)

(11)   The definition of courage in (1) is incorrect (199E11). (From 10)

This analysis of the argument resolves the ambiguity of the copula in (10) and all of the premises from which it is deduced, construing the copula as expressing identity throughout. This is certainly what it must express at (9), "knowledge of all good and evil is ... the whole of [virtue]," for what is to be concluded is the *identity of courage with the whole of virtue.* Here the copula cannot be ambiguous as between identifying and non-identifying predication: it must mean

---

[10] This analysis was adumbrated in the 2nd edn. of my *Platonic Studies* (1981: 443–5), superseding the earlier one in the 1st edn. of that book. For the present one I am indebted directly to Alan Code.

unambiguously the former. For (10) is understood to be the contradictory of (2); hence the copula cannot express mere interentailment, as has sometimes been assumed.[11] This cannot be how Socrates understands (9), for if it were he would not be taking (8) and (9) to entail (10), the contradictory of (2): there is no contradiction in supposing that courage is a part of virtue which is interentailing with each of the other parts of virtue and with the whole of it, as Socrates expressly does in the *Protagoras*.[12]

So to derive (10) by valid inference from its premises we must have identities in all the propositions from which it has been concluded. This we clearly have in premise (1): "knowledge of things which are fearful and confidence-sustaining" had been proposed by Nicias as a definition stating the true answer to "What is courage?" (194E11–195A1). And Socrates believes that to give a correct answer to "What is the *F*?"[13] is to give a defining formula which states "the very thing" (ὅπερ) the *F* is[14] or, equivalently, states "the essence [of the *F*] – what it [sc. the *F*] is";[15] in Plato's earlier dialogues, no less than those of his middle period, "the essence of *F*" and "the *F*" name the identical entity.[16] Moreover, that "knowledge of fearful and confidence-sustaining things" had been taken by Socrates in the *Protagoras* to be the essence of courage we can tell from the

---

[11] As in Friedländer, 1964: 47, and Gulley, 1968: 158–61.

[12] 329E4: if one has any virtue then "of necessity" one will have all the virtues. The same doctrine in Aristotle's view that all the moral virtues are inseparable (*N.E.* 1145a1–2) and in the Stoic doctrine of the interentailment (ἀντακολουθία) of the virtues (von Arnim, *SVF* III, pp. 44–5: so Zeno and Chrysippus in opposition to Aristo, *ibid.* pp. 62.1–8 and 62.20–63.10).

[13] Often called "the What-is-X? question" (after Richard Robinson, 1953: 49 *et passim*). "What is the *F*?" is preferable on two counts. It avoids the use of a variable whose values in modern logic are normally not abstract terms but concrete individuals. And it mirrors the grammatical structure of the idiom Socrates frequently uses to pose the question, where an adjective is transformed into a grammatical substantive by being cast into its articular neuter form.

[14] *Ch.* 160E4–5.

[15] *M.* 72B1–2, ἐρομένου μελίττης περὶ οὐσίας ὅτι ποτ' ἐστίν, where ὅτι ποτ' ἐστίν is in epexegetic apposition to οὐσίας and is a periphrasis for it. (On periphrases for οὐσία in Socratic dialogues see Thompson, 1901: 256.) In *Eu.* 11A too it is made clear that to answer "What is piety?" one must state the essence of piety.

[16] To assume with Allen, 1970: 103, n. 1, that "there is a distinction between the essence, X-ness, and the essence *of* X-ness" (his emphasis) would require Socrates to multiply entities *praeter necessitatem*. The only reason Allen gives for it (*loc. cit.*) is that "the question, 'What is X-ness?' must be answered by a defining formula of the essence, X-ness." But so must the question, "What is the essence of X-ness?", as is clear at *Eu.* 11A: "What is the essence of piety?" and "What is piety?" are the same question.

way he had derived the answer to "What is courage?" in that dialogue. He had reached it by deducing it (*Pr.* 360c) from the proposition that "ignorance of the things which are and are not fearful is *that because of which* (δι' ὅ) cowards are cowardly"; hence, conversely, knowledge of what is and is not fearful is that because of which the brave are brave. And we know that for Socrates "that because of which" *F* things are *F* is the essence of the *F*.[17] On this ground too we are assured that Socrates holds that premise (1) of the *TAL* is a strict identity: its predicate-term states the essence of courage.

At (3) there is no difficulty in assuring ourselves that here too the connective is meant to express identity. That the copula does have this force in "fear is expectation of future evil" (198b8–9) can be inferred from the form in which the phrase "expectation of evil" is related to "fear" at *Pr.* 358d5–e1. There Socrates asks his interlocutors if they call (καλεῖτε) "fear or dread" (εἴτε φόβον εἴτε δέος)[18] "the very thing" (ὅπερ) he too would call by that phrase. And we know that for Socrates the answer to "What is the *F*?" and "What is *called* the *F*?" is the same.[19] So when Socrates says that "expectation of evil" is what would be called "fear" he implies unambiguously that he takes the phrase to be an acceptable answer to "What is fear?",[20] thereby taking the phrase to state the essence of fear. Since (4), "expected evils/goods are future evils/goods," is a truism, the force of the connective in (3) is retained when it is conjoined with (4) to yield (5). At (6) too the force of the connective must be the same since (6) follows directly from the conjunction of (1) and (5).

---

[17] So e.g. at *Eu.* 10E–11A.

[18] He indicates (358e1–2) that the difference in meaning between the two words is negligible for his purposes.

[19] Because for him the two questions, calling for the same answer, are interchangeable in appropriate contexts. Thus at *La.* 192a1–b3 he starts with the first ("... if I were asking 'What is quickness [in all the cases he proceeds to enumerate]?'") and then shifts to the second ("If someone were to ask me, 'S. what would you say is what you call "quickness" in all these cases?' ..."), offering now the very answer he thinks required to answer the first. Again, at *M.* 74b–e, the question is first posed as "What is figure?" (74b5) and then asked again as "What is that whose name is 'figure'?" (74e11).

[20] And he appears to be so understood by Aristotle (καὶ τὸν φόβον ὁρίζονται προσδοκίαν κακοῦ, *N.E.* 1115a9) in a context which suggests that Socrates is the unnamed sponsor of the definition: Aristotle proceeds, again without naming Socrates, to object to the enormous widening of the application of "courage" whose *locus classicus* is *La.* 191c7–e2. Repeating three of its examples (courage displayed in poverty, illness, perils at sea), he remarks that only κατὰ μεταφοράν can the noble term "courage" be applied to these lusterless cases.

But what of (7)? Recognizing that this premise is far from self-evident and may even appear counter-intuitive, Socrates argues for it (198D–E). His point may be made clearer by an example. If a given proposition – say, that death would be better than dereliction of duty in the battle tomorrow – constitutes knowledge of good and evil, the truth of the proposition would be unaffected if "tomorrow" were replaced by "today" or by "yesterday" or by an expression referring to any other occasion in the past. The grounds of the proposition's truth would be the same; so the proposition would be tenselessly true. Since this is undoubtedly what he means, then, since Socrates holds that "knowledge of the same things, be they future or circumstanced in any other way [with respect to time] is the same knowledge" (*La.* 199B6–7),[21] it would be a tautology that knowledge of the same truth is the same knowledge.

Hence we have an identity at (8) too, for this proposition follows directly from (6) and (7). Then (10) follows trivially from (9), on the premise[22] that if x is a "part" of y, x is not identical with the whole of y, for y contains, in addition to x, other parts as well which, taken together, constitute the whole of y. Thus the conclusion that (2) is false is a valid inference.

(B)   Is premise (2) the refutand?

This unusual interpretation of the logical structure of the argument, first suggested casually by Santas,[23] was then adopted in all seriousness (without reference to Santas) and argued for in a paper by Penner[24] and, soon after, received influential support in Taylor's commentary on the *Protagoras*[25] and in Irwin's *Plato's Moral Theory*.[26] In Penner, Taylor, and Irwin this interpretation is predicated on

---

[21] Socrates takes knowledge to be individuated by its object (by what it is knowledge *of*), not by the subjective state of the person who has that knowledge. Only on this assumption could he hold that "all of virtue is knowledge" (*Pr.* 361B5–6): since he believes that the virtues are the same in all human beings (*M.* 73A–C), he would have to hold that the knowledge which constitutes a given virtue must be the same knowledge in all persons who have that virtue.

[22] Though implicit at this point in the argument, it had been made fully explicit earlier on: "You know that at the start of the argument we considered courage as a part of virtue... And you too gave your answer [about courage] as a part of virtue, there being other parts as well (ὄντων δὴ καὶ ἄλλων μερῶν [genitive absolute with epexegetic force]) which, taken all together, are called 'virtue'" (198A1–5).

[23] Santas, 1971: 202–3.   [24] 1973: 60–2.   [25] 1976: 107.   [26] 1977: 302, n. 62.

the assumption that the doctrine of the "unity of the virtues" in the
Protagoras is an affirmation of their *identity*.[27] I have previously[28]
pointed out that this interpretation will not square with the textual
evidence; it can only be maintained in defiance of what is said
by Socrates in Plato's earlier dialogues.[29] To regurgitate my arguments would be a boring redundancy. But since their claims
bear so directly on my continuing interpretation of the *TAL* I
must recall them summarily, directing attention to those parts of
Plato's text which make it entirely clear that they allow no other
option.

To suppose that Socrates is represented as offering an argument
which refutes premise (2) would be, in the first place, inconsistent
with the fact that in the *Laches* this premise articulates a doctrine
which Socrates introduces *in propria persona* and persuades each of his
interlocutors to accept.[30] He leads Laches to it at the start of his
discussion with him, before the question "What is courage?" has
been broached:

T2 *La.* 190c8–d8:   "Let us not, most excellent man, inquire right away about
the whole of virtue – this might be too big a job; let us first see if we are in a
position to have knowledge of one of its parts ... So which of the parts of virtue
shall we select? Is it not clear that it should be that [part of virtue] to which
training in fighting in armor[31] is conducive? In most people's view this is
courage ... So, Laches, let us first tackle this question: what *is* courage?"

Thus that courage is a "part" of virtue, stated clearly by Socrates,
and accepted unquestioningly by Laches, is the explicit presupposi-
tion of the dialogue's first elenctic investigation of the nature of
courage. It so remains in its second, when Nicias becomes the answerer. Socrates reminds him of it at laborious length:

---

[27] Taylor (1976: 107): "Plato sees nothing objectionable in the thesis that the different virtues
have the same *logos*." In a later paper (1982: 115), reaffirming his earlier view, he represents Socrates as holding that "each *arete* is identical with every other and with goodness as
such." Similarly Irwin (1977: *loc. cit.*): "all the virtues are the same virtue."

[28] Vlastos 1981: 418–23, "Socrates on 'the parts of virtue.'" Translated into French, this
essay is included in Canto-Sperber, 1991: 205–12.

[29] To this rebuttal there has been no response from Penner, Taylor, or Irwin.

[30] Thus its status in elenctic argument is radically different from a premise introduced by the
interlocutor and targeted for refutation by Socrates.

[31] Whose value for the acquisition of courage had just been discussed: conceded by Nicias
(181d–182d), rejected by Laches (182d–184c).

T3 *La.* 197E10–198A9:   "And you too Nicias, tell us again from the beginning. You do know that at the start of the discusssion [with Laches] we were investigation courage as a part of virtue? ... And you too, did you not give your answer [to 'What is courage?'] as a part [of virtue], there being other parts as well, which, taken all together, are called 'virtue'? ... Do you have in view the same parts as I? For I call [parts of virtue] temperance and justice and certain others of that sort in addition to courage (πρὸς ἀνδρείᾳ). Don't you too?"

Socrates makes it clear that in speaking of courage as "a part" of virtue he means that there are "other parts" of virtue "in addition" to courage, none of them identical with the whole of virtue or with any of the other parts.[32] How Taylor thinks this can be squared with his view that Socrates believes that "each *arete* is identical with every other and with goodness as such"[33] is unknown: there is no allusion to T3 in his book or in the paper which reaffirms the view.

Moreover, the same conception of the relation of the specific virtues to virtue reappears in the *Meno*, where it is spelled out at greater length and is explicated as the relation of specific figures to figure and of specific colors to color:

T4 *Meno* 74D5–E2:   "Since you call these many [figures] by the same name[34] and say that none of them *is* [i.e. is identical with] figure, these being even contrary to one another, there is something which covers the round no less than the straight, something you call 'figure,' and say that the round is a figure no less than the straight."

Socrates could hardly have made it clearer that courage could no more be identical with justice and with virtue as such than round could be identical with straight and with figure as such.

T4, like T3, passes unnoticed by Taylor in his book and then again in his paper on the *Euthyphro*, though directly relevant, since it is flatly irreconcilable with his claim that for Socrates "the different *aretai* have the same *logos*":[35] T4 shows that Socrates could no more allow the same *logos* for, say, justice and courage, than for round and straight. The same omission of any notice of T3 and T4 had marked

---

[32] He is using "part" to mean what logicians nowadays call a "proper part." This is what "part" *tout court* is commonly used to mean in Greek as it certainly is in ordinary English speech (the primary sense of "part" in the *O.E.D.* is "some but not all of a thing or number of things").

[33] Taylor, cited in n. 27 above.

[34] I.e. you call each of them "[a] figure."

[35] Taylor, cited in n. 27 above.

Penner's presentation of the view. It is only Irwin (1977: 304–5), maintaining here as usual an eagle eye for textual evidence bearing on his interpretations, who does recognize the *prima facie* contradiction between the identity of the virtues with one another and with virtue, on one hand, and what Socrates says in the *Meno*, on the other. But he thinks the conflict easily resolved:

M. 78D–79C[36] does not (as Vlastos thinks) show that Socrates recognizes parts of virtue; he simply allows Meno this view, to refute him . . .

In other words, that justice is to virtue as is round to figure and white to color, is *not* Socratic doctrine but a dialectical ploy: the whole of the elaborate exposition of justice as *a* virtue (ἀρετή τις) and *therefore* not identical with the whole of virtue but only with one of its parts[37] is a sham designed to fool the interlocutor and lower his defenses against refutation. Nowhere else in his discussion of Socratic argument does Irwin represent Socrates as making-believe what he does not believe in order to soften up an interlocutor for refutation. That he should find it necessary to make Socrates stoop to such tactics in this single passage shows up the weakness of the view he is trying to shore up. When we dismiss it, as we should, we are left with a passage expounding a syntactic distinction between each of the specific virtues and virtue (ἀρετή τις vs. ἀρετή), matching the semantic distinction between a proper part and the whole to which it belongs, which leaves no doubt that Socrates will have none of the conception of the identity of the virtues with one another and with virtue which Penner, Taylor, and Irwin have ascribed to him. That this whole passage should hail from the *Meno*, a dialogue much later than the *Laches*, is not less but rather more relevant to the proposal that premise (2) is meant to be the refutand in the *TAL*: Plato could hardly put into Socrates' mouth in a later Socratic dialogue acceptance and elaborate exposition of a doctrine which Socrates had formally refuted in an earlier one.

---

[36] I do not know why he mentions only this segment of the discussion in the *M.*, ignoring the fact that the exposition of the relation of each of the specific virtues to one another and to virtue begins at 73A9 and includes T3, to which Irwin makes no reference.
[37] *M.* 73D9ff.

III CONCLUSIONS

In my previous book on Socrates I blocked out the hypothesis on which my whole interpretation of Plato's dialogues depends: Plato makes Socrates say in any given dialogue "whatever *he* – Plato – thinks *at the time of writing* would be the most reasonable thing for Socrates to be saying just then in expounding and defending his own philosophy." On this hypothesis we have no option but to regard the *Laches* as composed after the *Protagoras*. For in the former he displays a lively awareness of the fact that when courage is defined as "knowledge of what is fearful and confidence-sustaining" the content of "knowledge" has to be moral, in contradistinction to technical, knowledge. If Plato had reached this awareness when he was writing the *Protagoras* he could hardly have maintained that those who were skilled in diving into wells, in cavalry-fighting and peltastry would be made not only more confident, but *braver* by their superior technical skill, which he knows to be false when writing the *Laches*, using those same three examples to reinforce the point that the "wise endurance" which manifests courage cannot be of the same order as that displayed by financiers, doctors, and military men in the exercise of their professional skills. And if the *Laches* is the later of the two dialogues, then so must be its refutation of the definition of "courage" established and used against the sophist in the *Protagoras*. We have then no choice but to conclude that when writing the *Laches* he had come to see that "knowledge of what is fearful and confidence-sustaining" cannot constitute a *definition* of "courage": it may still be accepted as stating an important truth about that virtue, but cannot be taken as capturing the *essence* – the necessary *and sufficient* condition of the courageous disposition.

To be sure, we could form a different hypothesis of Plato's intent in composing his dialogues. Thus if we suppose that what he meant to produce is vignettes of Socratic biography, none of the foregoing considerations would require us to suppose that the *Laches* was composed after the *Protagoras*. There is no cogent reason why a biographer should compose different episodes in his subject's life in the order in which they had occurred. In that case, he might well have chosen to write his portrayal of the more youthful, less mature, Socrates in the *Protagoras* after having pictured him in a previously written dialogue as well aware of the fact that the knowledge of fearful and confidence-sustaining things which formed the essence of courage could not be craft-knowledge such as that possessed by divers, cavalrymen, and peltasts. It is only if we proceed on the hypothesis that Plato is writing philosophy, not biography, that the order of composition has to be the same as the order of growing insight. Once Plato had come by the insight that moral knowledge, in contrast to technical knowledge, which forms the essence of courage and of the other virtues (an insight he would continue to expound in other dialogues beside the *Laches*: the *Charmides*, the *Gorgias*, the *Euthydemus*), it would be unintelligible that he should want to make Socrates revert to a position which allows him to argue that technical skill will of itself make men braver than they would be without it.

The same considerations tell also against a third hypothesis which is being currently defended by Charles Kahn. Rejecting, quite rightly, the biographical intent of Plato's dialogues, Kahn argues for a "proleptic" hypothesis: that five of Plato's earlier dialogues – *Laches*, *Charmides*, *Lysis*, *Euthyphro*, and *Protagoras* – are written in that order and that their purpose is "to prepare the minds of [Plato's] audience ... for the reception of his mature philosophy" which will be expounded in the dialogues of Plato's middle periods. So large a hypothesis raises a multitude of questions which call for separate treatment.[38] Here I must content myself with querying the assumption that the *Protagoras* was composed after the other four. As I have argued in the foregoing, this founders on the fact of which Kahn appears to be unaware, namely that in the *Protagoras* Plato's Socrates uses an argument which he could not have used if he had already recognized the contrast between moral and technical knowledge which is revealed in the *Laches* and again in the *Charmides* and in the *Gorgias* too (which Kahn would have us think earlier than any dialogue in the above quintet) and also in the, still later, *Euthydemus*.

---

[38] Some of them are pursued systematically by McPherran, 1990.

EPILOGUE:
SOCRATES AND VIETNAM[1]

The lines that close the death-scene in the *Phaedo* are well known:

"Such, Echecrates, was the end of our companion – a man, we might say, who of all those we came to know was the best and, in any case, the wisest and the most just."

Was Socrates really as good as that? I have never seen this question raised anywhere in the vast literature on him. I raise it in full view of the fact that throughout his corpus Plato presents his teacher as a man without a peer in three of the virtues most honored among the Greeks – courage, *sophrosyne*, and piety. Plato is as emphatic on the third as on the other two, making it the crux of the defense against the charge of impiety on which Socrates was to be condemned to death: Socrates' practice of philosophy had been itself a lifelong exercise of piety, obedience to the god of Delphi who had "ordered him to philosophize, examining himself and others."[2] Plato makes it clear that it was just because of unflinching obedience to that divine command that Socrates had been convicted: had he been willing to propose self-muzzlement as an alternative he could have been acquitted.

So in the case of those three qualities Socrates' character is flaw-less, granite-solid in Plato's portrait of him. But what of the one that forms the punch-word in the epitaph: "and *most just*"? Plato feels so sure that on this score too the record is perfect that he has Socrates say he will face divine judgment in the nether world confident that

---

[1] An Address at the Graduation of candidates in Classical and Modern Languages and Literatures at the University of California at Berkeley on 20 May 1987.
[2] *Ap.* 28E.

he "had never wronged anyone, man or god."[3] Suppose we were assured that he had never defaulted on an obligation to a single person. We could still ask: What of his obligations to his city? Does Plato leave us satisfied that here too Socrates is above reproach? I submit that he does not.

As a citizen of Athens, Socrates may be judged by that peculiarly Athenian standard voiced by Pericles in his Funeral Oration in Thucydides:

"For we alone regard someone who takes no part in politics not as one who sticks to his own business but as a man who is good for nothing."[4]

What Socrates had made his own business throughout his life had been elenctic soul-saving. This had filled his life, day in, day out, leaving no time for what would count as "doing politics" (*prattein ta politika*) in Athens, i.e. taking part in the debates in the Assembly and other functions where public policy was shaped. From what the Athenians would have counted as *prattein ta politika* Socrates had conscientiously abstained. (Refusal to concur with the illegal motion to try the ten generals en masse or to obey the order of the Thirty to help arrest an innocent man for execution would not have counted as such.) So from Pericles' point of view Socrates is "good for nothing." But we need not rest content with that. Let us consider for ourselves what staying out of politics had meant for Socrates at two fateful points of Athenian history.

In March 415 B.C. the Assembly debates whether or not Athens should give aid to the Segestans – a petty ally in far-off Sicily, at the westernmost edge of the Greek world. To comply would be to open a new front in the intermittent war with Sparta, drawing Syracuse into it, a new belligerent, a bigger, richer, more formidable antagonist than any so far arrayed against Athens. Can she afford it? Advocates of expansionist imperialism clamor for it with Alcibiades, brilliant and unscrupulous as ever, at their head. Nicias, older, more conservative, urges caution, dwelling on the huge investment this engagement so far from home would require, while Sparta, Corinth, and the rest are at Athens' doorstep, ready to pounce. Good sense

---

[3] *G.* 522D.   [4] *Hist.* 2.40.2.

is strongly on Nicias' side. But imperial greed and pride prevail. Athens goes headlong into the adventure. A vast budget is voted and, not long after, the greatest expeditionary force ever assembled in Greece sails for Syracuse. The outcome? Total disaster for Athens. Of the 45,000–50,000 soldiers and sailors sent out from Athens and her allies only 7,000 survive and they enter Syracuse as captives of war, condemned to a fate which for many of them was scarcely better than death, herded in stone quarries, where many would die of wounds, disease, deprivation of food and water, in filth and stench, denied facilities to dispose of their waste and bury their dead.

Was Socrates present in the Assembly that day the disastrous vote was taken? We do not know. But we can infer securely that if present he kept his mouth shut. For when he reviews his political past at his trial fourteen years later he pleads guilty to the reproach that throughout his life he "had not mounted the rostrum to advise the state."[5] The reason he gives is surprising:

"You know that if I had tried to do politics long ago I would have perished long ago and done no good to you or to myself."[6]

The defeatism of this retrospective judgment is unwarranted: why discount the effect of cool sardonic comment from Athens' gadfly to bring down a degree or two the overheated atmosphere of the debate? In any case, considering how desperate was his city's need for sober advice, would it not have been his duty to do whatever he could, little or much, to make the voice of reason heard, regardless of consequences to himself?

The same question arises with greater force on another occasion, when Athens needed to be saved not just from a strategic blunder but from a moral outrage. Mytilene, a non-tributary member of the Athenian League, had defected to Sparta and had been subdued after a long costly siege. Furious that a long-standing ally of theirs should have deserted, fearing that other members of her League would do the same, the Athenians were minded to decree exemplary punishment. Cleon proposes a sentence of unprecedented ferocity: all adult citizens of Mytilene to be executed; all women and children

---

[5] *Ap.* 31C.   [6] *Ibid.* 31D.

sold into slavery. His motion passes by a narrow margin and a warship is dispatched to have the order executed. Fortunately this was not to be Athens' last word:

On the next day came some change of heart and second thoughts; it seemed savage and monstrous to destroy a whole city instead of those who had been responsible.[7]

The Assembly is convoked again, the question is reopened. The speakers are the same as before. This time Thucydides gives a good idea of what they said. Sticking to his previous proposal Cleon, "most violent and most persuasive of the citizens at the time,"[8] supports it on the ground of both expediency and justice – the justice of the *lex talionis*. The spokesman for the other side, Diodotus, an otherwise unknown Athenian, hardly makes the most of his case. First he says he will not appeal to justice but only to imperial interest: he argues, not too convincingly, that to punish the people as harshly as their oligarchic rulers, architects of the defection, would jeopardize Athens' best asset in the war, the sympathy of the democrats in each of the allied and subject cities. He then comes around to justice after all but fails to play his strongest card: if the Athenians wished to retaliate, as Cleon recommends, they could not do it justly by a punishment so grossly disproportionate to the crime; to exterminate the Mytilenians would have been not an eye for an eye, but a life for an eye. His side prevails by the slenderest of margins. Another warship is dispatched, reaching Mytilene just in time to prevent the massacre.

It may seem incomprehensible that a man like Socrates, who would rather lose his life than connive in an injustice to a single person should nonetheless have kept silent when his own participation might have saved Athens from the vilest crime yet perpetrated in war between Greek states, and should have kept silent again and again when Athens was to commit just such a crime against Torone, Scione, and Melos. Is there any way of understanding how a rational man of exemplary rectitude could have failed to speak in exercise of his civic rights when acts of that ilk by the city he loved so much hung in the balance? We may get a glimmering of insight into

---

[7] Thuc. *Hist.* 3.36.4.   [8] *Ibid.* 3.36.6.

it if we recall that all of Socrates' energies are committed single-mindedly to that one thing he felt his god commanded him to do: "to live philosophizing, examining himself and others." Addressing a multitude even in the best of causes would not have been what Socrates understands by "philosophizing"; only one-to-one elenctic argument could measure up to the specifications of what Socrates understands by that: anything else would be diversionary from that god-ordered mission to his city.

However unconvincing that apologia might have seemed to most of Socrates' contemporaries, however unconvincing it might still seem to most of us today, there is one kind of man who can resonate with some degree of sympathy for it – the kind of man I have been through 56 years of academic employment. A man bent on scholarly work in present-day academia has at least this much in common with the Socrates of this address: vocational dedication. Like Socrates the scholar must reserve his energies for work for which he is uniquely qualified by talent, training, and application, pledged to search for truth in his own discipline with its own special tools and objectives. And he must see this as a full-time job – full-time plus. To do it he needs time, more time, and again still more. He never has enough. His place in the university is won by means of a parallel vocation which also demands and deserves dedication and could claim all of his working hours all by itself, pressing for time to get its own work done, insisting on it in a far more immediate and urgent way than does his research. His teaching deadlines are made for him and he is held to them daily by the clock, while research deadlines are of his own choosing and there is no one but himself to hold him to them: they are the ones that give when something has to give in his work-schedule. When further demands are made on him, as they well may in the self-governing community a university is privileged to be, it is again his research-time that has to give. This is what makes it possible for me to understand, if not excuse, in Socrates what would otherwise have seemed blatant dereliction of duty or worse, a crazy quirk, a psychological aberration.

I started teaching in Canada in 1931 in the depths of the Great Depression which had hit there even worse than here. I joined spontaneously the struggle for economic justice, becoming deeply involved in movements of protest. So research plans were crowded out. The ambitions with which I had left graduate school went by the board year after year. The first paper of any consequence I managed to produce for print appeared in 1939, eight years out of graduate school, by which time I would have been fired for sterility by almost every academic employer in this country. After the war came the move to the U.S. And here the problem that had bedevilled the first decade of my career – the havoc political and parapolitical work had caused my scholarship – was solved for me by the inadvertent kindness of the late unlamented Senator McCarthy. I was one of the beneficiaries of the fall-out from his persecutions. There was a file in the State Department on my record in Canada and I had entered the U.S. on sufferance. This was impressed on me by a summons to the Ithaca office of the F.B.I. (I was teaching at Cornell) which made me wonder if I was in for some sort of criminal investigation: the interview began with the warning that anything I said could be held against me. This did not cramp my style, for I had nothing to hide. But it did put a damper on political engagements I might have contemplated while an alien here. So all such designs were laid to rest and energies previously siphoned off in non-scholarly speaking and writing could now be kept for research in classical philosophy. My scholarship prospered.

Then came Vietnam. Its impact on me had been prepared by what I had seen students do just before to confound their elders' inaction. The first was what black students had done in the South to challenge segregation there and what other students nearer home (I was now at Princeton) did for that cause, like spending a summer in Mississippi registering black voters. The second was the Free Speech Movement in Berkeley whose ripples reached every campus, even silent-generation strongholds, such as Princeton had been all through the fifties and early sixties. But what ended the cop-out from dissent for me, as for so many of my colleagues, was Vietnam. Seeing my students and my own son required by law to become uniformed killers in a cause which they despised put an end to my qualms. Though still a guest, precariously domiciled, in this country, I saw my scruples melt away. When someone had to move the anti-Vietnam resolution at a meeting of the Eastern Division of the

American Philosophical Association in December 1966, and it was pointed out to me that this would be done most fittingly by the retiring president of the Division, which happened to be myself, I accepted the assignment without the slightest hesitation. I would gladly do the same in similar circumstances today in protest against the current U.S. intervention by proxy in Central America, funding mercenaries to terrorize impoverished peasants, people innocent of any crime except loyalty to their own entirely legitimate government.

So what can I offer you by way of the avuncular advice expected on such occasions[9] from an older scholar to fledgling ones? All I can do is make a small return of what the old have learned from the courage of the young in recent decades. I ask you to accept what Socrates never did: the concurrent, not easily harmonized, claims on us of the intellectual's lonely search for truth and the corporate struggle for justice. Both claims are valid, both morally inescapable. We must respond to both. To give up scholarship would be not only imprudent but ethically indefensible; it would be to default on what we owe the nation and humanity. Yet neither dare we shirk our part, great or small, against injustice. To do so would be to forfeit self-respect. Socrates kept his by an ethic which cannot be ours – a simplistic one, recognizing only wrongs by persons to persons, ignoring that social dimension of morality in which wrongs he abhors may be done by the city he loves – wrongs as monstrous as the one Athens all but decreed for Mytilene and executed not long after against Scione, Torone, and Melos.

In the obituary for Gunnar Myrdal in the New York Times[10] we read that this man who joined with rare effectiveness social intelligence to social passion kept close to his desk this quotation from Lincoln:

To sin by silence when they should protest makes cowards of men.

Socrates has been and always will be my philosophical hero. But great and good as he certainly was, he would have been a greater and better man, wiser and *more just*, if that truth had enlightened his moral vision.

[9] cf. n. 1 above. [10] 18 June 1987.

ADDITIONAL NOTES

1.1 THE CHRONOLOGICAL ORDER OF THE DIALOGUES

The chronological order of those works of Plato which I accept as genuine (on grounds which I have explained and defended at the start of chapter 2, section 1 in *Socrates: Ironist and Moral Philosopher* [hereafter "*Socrates*"]) is as follows.

(1) The Earlier Dialogues (listed in alphabetical order): *Apology, Charmides, Crito, Euthydemus, Euthyphro, Gorgias, Hippias Major, Hippias Minor, Ion, Laches, Lysis, Menexenus, Protagoras, Republic* I. I take the *Lysis, Euthydemus, Hippias Major* to follow the *Gorgias* (see the Appendix to chapter 1). The *Gorgias* is the only one of the earlier dialogues preceding this trio. It precedes the *Menexenus* as well, and all the above-mentioned works precede the *Meno*, which marks the point of transition from the earlier to the middle dialogues (so I have listed it neither under (1) nor under (2)); for what is groundbreakingly new in the *Meno* see *Socrates*, chapter 4, comment on texts quoted as T12–T21.

(2) The Dialogues of the Middle Period (listed in probable chronological order): *Cratylus, Phaedo, Symposium, Republic* II–X, *Phaedrus, Parmenides, Theaetetus.*

(3) The Dialogues of the Later Period (listed in probable chronological order): *Timaeus, Critias, Sophist, Politicus, Philebus, Laws.* For the place of the *Timaeus* in this order see *Socrates*, additional note 2.6.

1.2 ELENCHUS VS. ERISTIC

The confusion of elenchus with eristic pervades much of the modern literature. It runs through Ryle's description of "the Socratic

Method" in his article on Plato in *The Encyclopedia of Philosophy* (1967)
and also in his *Plato's Progress* (1966), where the elenctic arguments
in Plato's earlier dialogues are represented as "specimens of eristic
contests." The misconception is abetted by a blatant disregard of the
"say what you believe" requirement (discussed in chapter 1 above),
which is ignored even in the admirable essay by Paul Moraux, "La
joute dialectique d'après le huitième livre des *Topiques*" (1968), an
incomparably more exact discussion, which notes carefully some
other points of difference between Socratic elenchi and the "dialectical jousts" in Aristotle.

Similar disregard of that requirement accounts for other con-
flations of Socratic dialectic with eristic, beginning with George
Grote.[1] Using "eristic" with culpable looseness, he makes no mention of the "say only what you believe" requirement, so fundamental for elenchus, in his discussion of "the real contrast" between
Socrates and the *outré* eristics in the *Euthydemus*. This is what makes it
possible for Grote to say that in the *Protagoras* Socrates is "decidedly
more Eristic" than the sophist: he is using "eristic" to mean "con-
tentious." Contentiousness in argument is indeed one of Socrates'
failings (for which Plato, in retrospect, gently reproaches him in the
Theaetetus).[2] But in spite of such personal lapses on the part of its
human instrument, elenchus remains a method of searching for the
truth, which eristic is not, but only a method (or set of methods – a
whole bag of tricks) for winning arguments, regardless of whether or
not you think what you are arguing for is true (cf. the excellent description of eristic in Kerferd, 1981: 62–3), while in elenchus the aim
of "coming to know what is true and what is false" is paramount (*G.*
505E; cf. *Ch.* 165C and *G.* 486E).

For Aristotle's recognition of "saying what you believe" in Socratic
dialectic, see *Top.* 160b19–22: the answerer is not just "maintaining
a position for the sake of argument (ὡς λόγου χάριν ὑπέχοντα), but
saying what he believes (ἀλλ' ὡς τὰ δοκοῦντα λέγοντα)." Though
Socrates is not named, the examples (that "the good is pleasure"
and "to suffer injustice is better than to do it") show that Aristotle is
alluding to Socrates' argument against Callicles in the *Gorgias*.

---

[1] 1865: I, 535.   [2] 167E–168A. See comment on this passage in *Socrates*, p. 155 with n. 92.

1.3 ON *GORGIAS* 508E–509A

In chapter 3 of *Socrates* (p. 84) I called attention to "the most paradoxical aspect" of Socrates' disavowal of knowledge, "its unique, absolutely unparalleled, feature" – that it is made in the face of the assertion that he can prove his theses true. This is displayed in the words with which Socrates looks back on his argument against Callicles and ponders its upshot:

G. 508E–509A: "These things, having been shown in our earlier arguments to be as I state them [a] are clamped down and bound, if I may put it so bluntly, with arguments of adamant and iron, or so one would think – arguments which [b1] if you, or someone still younger and more vigorous than yourself, does not undo, it will not be possible for anyone to speak otherwise than I do and speak correctly. For my position is always the same: [c] I do not know how these things are, yet nonetheless [b2] no one I have encountered has proved capable of speaking otherwise without making himself ridiculous – as has happened on this occasion."

At [a] Socrates claims to have *proved* his theses true. He does not use the word, but that this is what he means is made clear enough by his metaphor: one can hardly imagine a stronger image for the *proof* of a thesis than its being "clamped down and bound with arguments of adamant and iron." At [c] he says he does not *know* if his theses are true.[3] At [b1] and then again at [b2] we get an inkling of what he may mean by the paradoxical conjunction of the two claims: the claim at [a] is made subject to elenctic challenge at [b1]. Anyone who disputes his claim to have proved his theses true, is invited to "undo" those arguments of "adamant and iron," to "speak otherwise" without making himself "ridiculous" by being made to eat his words. So while the claim at [a] is as confident as it could be – Socrates accepts unwaveringly the truth of his theses, he does not hesitate to live by those theses, predicating his life on their truth – yet it is provisional, subject to constant reexamination by elenctic argument: explicitly at [b1], implicitly at [b2], it is said to stand *unless* someone can prove it false by the method Socrates has used to prove it true.

---

[3] He had admitted as much a little earlier: "For I do not speak as one who has knowledge" (506A).

3.1 PRESUMPTIVE MORAL KNOWLEDGE

What would Socrates do with the moral commonplaces of his age – general propositions like "virtue is good," "virtuous action is fine (καλόν)," "temperance is a virtue," or examples of virtuous action which are regarded as utterly uncontroversial like "doing good to one's friends is good and fine"? Would he consider them questionable until each of them had been subjected to elenctic testing? His procedure shows that he would not. Thus when Laches says, "If someone wants to stay in the ranks to fight the enemy, you know well that he is brave" (*La.* 190E), Socrates agrees instantly: "You speak well." He does not reject Laches' claim to know that this would be true, since this would be a standard example of courage. A proposition of this sort, and hundreds like it which form the staple of what the vast majority of his fellows take as moral knowledge, Socrates would accept as *presumptive elenctic knowledge*. By so describing this and other commonplace cases of courage, we take due account of Burnyeat's point that the examples Socrates uses are not regarded as "little hard rocks of certainty":[4] they do not constitute knowledge$_C$; any of them are open to challenge *more elenctico*, and, if they survive elenctic testing, will be recognized as (non-presumptive) elenctic knowledge. Thus the counter-examples to Nicias' definition of "courage" in the *Laches* – notoriously "brave" animals, like lions and leopards which could not be credited with knowledge – are rebutted by being redescribed by Nicias (*La.* 197A–B) as cases of "daring" (τόλμα) rather than courage; when Laches grants the redescription, the proposed counter-examples are withdrawn.

A proposition like "justice is a virtue" would count as presumptive moral knowledge$_E$. If the interlocutor grants it, Socrates can use it as a premise in elenctic argument. But he does not present it as "a hard rock of certainty." No one is told that it is self-evidently true and cannot be doubted if there is good reason for doing so. Socrates does not rule out of court Thrasymachus when he denies outright that justice is a virtue, claiming that, on the contrary, it is "noble

---

[4] Burnyeat, 1977b.

simplemindedness (πάνυ γενναίαν εὐήθειαν)" (348c). When this kind of objection comes up Socrates meets it head-on: he takes it as a thesis that requires (and gets) elenctic refutation.

Thus in Socratic elenchus there is no appeal to "reputable truths" (ἔνδοξα) as "starting-points" (ἀρχαί) of moral knowledge. Both Socrates and Aristotle proceed on the basis of commonly granted, uncontroversial, truths. The difference is that Socrates does not give them the cognitively privileged status they get in Aristotle. For Socrates every proposition is open to elenctic challenge. He argues "peirastically," content to use as premises simply those propositions which the interlocutor, "saying what he believes," accepts: he argues "from the interlocutor's own beliefs" (ἐκ τῶν δοκούντων τῷ ἀποκρινομένῳ, Aristotle, *Soph. El.* 165b4–5).

BIBLIOGRAPHY

Allen, R. E. (1970). *Plato's "Euthyphro" and the Earlier Theory of Forms*, London & New York

Beversluis, John (1987). "Does Socrates Commit the Socratic Fallacy?," *American Philosophical Quarterly* 24: 211–23

Brandwood, Leonard (1976). *A Word Index to Plato*, Leeds

Brickhouse, Thomas & Smith, Nicholas D. (1984). "Vlastos on the Elenchus," *Oxford Studies in Ancient Philosophy* 2: 185–95

Burnet, John (1914). *Greek Philosophy*, Part 1. *Thales to Plato*, London

Burnyeat, M. F. (1977a). "Socratic Midwifery, Platonic Inspiration," *Bulletin of the Institute of Classical Studies* 24: 7–16

(1977b). "Examples in Epistemology: Socrates, Theaetetus and G. E. Moore," *Philosophy* 52: 381–98

(1981). "Aristotle on Understanding Knowledge," in *Aristotle on Science: The "Posterior Analytics*," ed. Enrico Berti, Padua, 97–139

Campbell, Lewis (1867). *The Sophistes and Politicus of Plato*, a revised text and English notes, Oxford

Canto-Sperber, Monique (1991). *Les Paradoxes de la connaissance: essais sur le Ménon de Platon*, recueillis et présentés par Monique Canto-Sperber, Paris

Cornford, F. M. (1935). *Plato's Theory of Knowledge. The Theaetetus and the Sophist of Plato*, translated with a running commentary, London

Demand, Nancy H. (1982). *Thebes in the Fifth Century: Heracles Resurgent*, London

Dodds, E. R. (1959). *Plato "Gorgias*," a revised text with introduction and commentary, Oxford

Dover, K. J. (1976). "The Freedom of the Intellectual in Greek Society," *Talanta* 7: 24–54

Frerejohn, Michael T. (1984). "Socratic Thought-Experiments and the Unity of Virtue Paradox," *Phronesis* 29: 105–22

Friedländer, Paul (1964). *Plato*, vol. II: *The Dialogues, First Period*, translated from the German by Hans Meyerhoff, New York

Geach, P. T. (1966). "Plato's *Euthyphro*: An Analysis and Commentary," *Monist* 50: 369–82; reprinted in P. T. Geach, *Logic Matters* (Oxford 1972) 31–44

Grote, George (1865). *Plato and the Other Companions of Sokrates*, vols. I–III, London

   (1906). *A History of Greece* [1st edn. 1846–56], Everyman edn., 12 vols., London

Gulley, Norman (1968). *The Philosophy of Socrates*, London

Guthrie, W. K. C. (1969). *A History of Greek Philosophy*, vol. III: *The Fifth-Century Enlightenment*, Cambridge

   (1975). *A History of Greek Philosophy*, vol. IV: *Plato, The Man and his Dialogues: Earlier Period*, Cambridge

Hackforth, R. (1933). *The Composition of Plato's Apology*, Cambridge

Hall, Roland (1967). "Dialectic" in *The Encyclopedia of Philosophy*, ed. Paul Edwards, New York

Irwin, Terence (1974). Review of Leo Strauss, *Xenophon's Socrates*, in *Philosophical Review* 83: 409–13

   (1977). *Plato's Moral Theory: The Early and Middle Dialogues*, Oxford

   (1979). *Plato: Gorgias*, translated with notes, Oxford

Kahn, Charles H. (1981). "Did Plato write Socratic dialogues?," *Classical Quarterly* 31: 305–20

Kerferd, G. B. (1981). *The Sophistic Movement*, Cambridge

Keulen, Hermann (1971). *Untersuchungen zu Platons "Euthydem,"* Klassisch-Philologische Studien Heft 37, Wiesbaden

Kidd, I. G. (1967). "Socrates" in *The Encyclopedia of Philosophy*, ed. Paul Edwards, New York

Kirk, G. S., Raven, J. E. & Schofield, M. (1983). *The Presocratic Philosophers*, 2nd edn., Cambridge

Kraut, Richard (1981). "Plato's *Apology* and *Crito*: Two Recent Studies," *Ethics* 91: 651–64

   (1983). "Comments on Gregory Vlastos, 'The Socratic Elenchus,'" *Oxford Studies in Ancient Philosophy* 1: 59–70

Lowrie, Walter (1938). *Kierkegaard*, Oxford

Maier, Heinrich (1913). *Sokrates: sein Werk und seine geschichtliche Stellung*, Tübingen

McDowell, John (1973). *Plato: Theaetetus*, translated with notes, Oxford

McPherran, Mark L. (1990). "Kahn on the Pre-Middle Platonic Dialogues: Comments on Charles Kahn, 'On the Relative Date of the *Gorgias* and the *Protagoras*,'" *Oxford Studies in Ancient Philosophy* 8: 211–36

Moore, J. M. (1975). *Aristotle and Xenophon on Democracy and Oligarchy*, London

Moraux, Paul (1968). "La joute dialectique d'après le huitième livre des *Topiques*," in *Aristotle on Dialectic: The Topics*, ed. G. E. L. Owen, Oxford, 277–311

Morrison, Donald (1987). "On Professor Vlastos' Xenophon," *Ancient Philosophy* 7: 9–22

Nozick, Robert (1981). *Philosophical Explanations*, Oxford

Ostwald, Martin (1969). *Nomos and the Beginnings of Athenian Democracy*, Oxford

Penner, Terry (1973). "The Unity of Virtues," *Philosophical Review* 82: 35–68

Polansky, Ronald M. (1985). "Professor Vlastos's Analysis of Socratic Elenchus," *Oxford Studies in Ancient Philosophy* 3: 247–59

Reeve, C. D. C. (1989). *Socrates in the "Apology," an essay on Plato's Apology of Socrates*, Indianapolis

Robinson, Richard (1953). *Plato's Earlier Dialectic*, 2nd edn., Oxford

Ross, W. D. (1924). *Aristotle's Metaphysics*, a revised text with introduction and commentary, vols. I-II, Oxford

(1951). *Plato's Theory of Ideas*, Oxford

Ryle, Gilbert (1966). *Plato's Progress*, Cambridge

(1967). "Plato" in *The Encyclopedia of Philosophy*, ed. Paul Edwards, New York

Santas, Gerasimos Xenophon (1971). "Socrates at Work on Virtue and Knowledge in Plato's *Laches*," in *The Philosophy of Socrates: A Collection of Critical Essays*, ed. Gregory Vlastos, New York, 177–208

(1972). "The Socratic Fallacy," *Journal of the History of Philosophy* 10: 127–41

(1979). *Socrates: Philosophy in Plato's Early Dialogues*, London

Schoplick, V. (1969). *Der platonische Dialog "Lysis,"* Augsburg

Shorey, Paul (1933). *What Plato Said*, Chicago

Sidgwick, H. (1872). "The Sophists," *Journal of Philology* 4: 288–307

Taylor, C. C. W. (1976). *Plato: Protagoras*, translated with notes, Oxford

(1982). "The End of the Euthyphro," *Phronesis* 27: 109–18

Thompson, E. Seymer (1901). *The Meno of Plato*, edited with Introduction, Notes, and Excursuses, London

Vlastos, G. (1956). *Plato's "Protagoras,"* translation by B. Jowett, extensively revised by Martin Ostwald, ed. with an Introduction, by Gregory Vlastos, New York

(1957–8). "The Paradox of Socrates," *Queen's Quarterly*, 64: 496–516, reprinted with slight changes in *The Philosophy of Socrates: A Collection of Critical Essays*, ed. Gregory Vlastos, New York, 1–21

(1973). *Platonic Studies*, Princeton

(1978). Review of H. Cherniss, *Selected Papers*, ed. by L. Tarán, in *American Journal of Philology* 99: 537–43

(1980). Review of Ellen & Neil Wood, *Class Ideology and Ancient Political Theory*, *Phoenix* 34: 347–52

(1981). *Platonic Studies*, 2nd edn., Princeton

(1983a). "The Socratic Elenchus," *Oxford Studies in Ancient Philosophy* 1: 27-58

(1983b). "Afterthoughts on the Socratic Elenchus," *Oxford Studies in Ancient Philosophy* 1: 71–4

(1983c). "The Historical Socrates and Athenian Democracy," *Political Theory* 11: 495–515

(1983d). Review of E. N. Platis, Οἱ κατήγοροι τοῦ Σωκράτη. Φιλολογική μελέτη (*The Accusers of Socrates. A Philological Study*), *American Journal of Philology* 104: 201–6

(1985). "Socrates' Disavowal of Knowledge," *Philosophical Quarterly* 35: 1–31

(1988). "Elenchus and Mathematics: A Turning Point in Plato's Philosophical Development," *American Journal of Philology* 109: 362–96

(1990). "Is the 'Socratic Fallacy' Socratic?," *Ancient Philosophy* 10: 1–16

(1991). *Socrates: Ironist and Moral Philosopher*, Cambridge and Ithaca

Woodruff, Paul (1982). *Plato, "Hippias Major,"* translated, with commentary and essay, Indianapolis and Oxford

(1983). Review of R. E. Allen, *Socrates and Legal Obligation*, in *Journal of the History of Philosophy* 21: 93–5

Zeller, E. (1885). *Socrates and the Socratic Schools*, translated from the third German edn. by Oswald J. Reichel, London

INDEX OF PASSAGES CITED

INDEX OF ANCIENT NAMES

INDEX OF MODERN SCHOLARS

INDEX OF GREEK WORDS